Self-Suffi

Natural
Remedies

Self-Sufficiency
Natural
Remedies

Melissa Corkhill

NEW
HOLLAND

First published in 2011 by New Holland Publishers (UK) Ltd
London • Cape Town • Sydney • Auckland

Garfield House	80 McKenzie Street	Unit 1	218 Lake Road
86–88 Edgware Rd	Cape Town 8001	66 Gibbes Street	Northcote
London W2 2EA	South Africa	Chatswood	Auckland
United Kingdom		NSW 2067	New Zealand
		Australia	

ISBN 978 1 84773 773 1

Publisher: Clare Sayer
Senior Editor: Emma Pattison
Designer: Peter Crump
Main illustrations: Michael Stones
All other artwork: e-Digital Design
Production: Laurence Poos

1 3 5 7 9 10 8 6 4 2

Reproduction by Pica Digital PTE Ltd, Singapore
Printed and bound in China by Toppan Leefung Printing Ltd

Publisher's Note
The natural remedies included in this book are not intended as a substitute for professional medical treatment. A physician should be consulted in all cases of medical concern and if symptoms arise that require medical diagnosis. Neither the author nor the publisher accept any responsibility or liability for any effects that may arise from following the advice given here.

CONTENTS

Getting started

Nature provides us with a wealth of natural remedies that can help to ease and soothe illnesses, ailments and common health complaints. The following pages contain all you need to know to begin treating yourself and your family by increasing your plant knowledge, putting together a herbal first aid kit and even growing your own medicine.

Introduction

I started this journey as a child, always fascinated by plants and intrigued at the natural remedies that my mother used to treat us when my brother, sister and I were ill. She had a huge collection of homeopathic remedies and through her treating us, I learnt about many of them, what they were made from and what symptoms they could be used to treat. I came to understand that a heavy cold could benefit from a dose of Pulsatilla, that a case of nerves before an exam was effectively treated using Gelsemium, and that a hot honey and lemon drink was the best remedy for a sore throat.

When my own children were born I started to use natural remedies to treat their illnesses and found that as they got older they were able to decide what remedy would work best for them. They instinctively know what plant will be most effective to help their bodies to heal. I have learned to trust their innate knowledge and at the time of writing none of us has seen a doctor for six years! We are our own doctors, which is a liberating feeling.

No one can know and understand your body better than you can. I like to do a body scan meditation every once in a while to give my body a chance to really let me know how it is feeling and any problem areas that need looking at. Simply lie down in a comfortable place where you can be sure that you won't be disturbed for at least 20 minutes. Bring your attention to your feet. Think about how they feel. Give your body time to respond, as you may not be used to focussing on individual parts in this way. If you can't decide how your feet are feeling first time, don't worry, simply move to your ankles and focus on them.

Slowly move up your body, thinking about how it is feeling, until you get to the head. You may have thoughts such as 'I'm tired; I feel confused; I feel stuck'. After you have worked through the whole body, sit up and jot down each of the messages from your body parts so that you have a reference to work with over the coming weeks. You can then refer to the advice given in this book to treat and heal any problem areas.

When parts of my body feel stiff or blocked, I use yoga and herbs to help me release the tension. Yoga is an incredible therapy for moving and releasing blockages that might go on to cause illness if allowed to build up. For example, I developed a benign lump in my breast two years ago and through the practice of yoga and use of natural remedies I managed to shift the blockage and now feel healthier than ever. (Remember you should always consult a doctor if you discover a lump in your breast or any other part of your body.)

In this book I will share remedies and techniques that I have used myself for decades and on my children for over ten years. Many of the recipes for healing lotions, infusions and tinctures are ones that we use regularly in our home. I hope that they will be useful for you to help you create optimum health for you and your family.

How to use this book

I have divided this book up into bodily systems, so you will find remedies for the respiratory system in one chapter and how to heal disorders of the digestive system in another (see list opposite). I prefer to work with the body as a whole rather than just the symptoms but for ease of use and understanding I have chosen to organise the book in this way. You may find that you need to look in more than one section to find a selection of treatments that work for you. For example if your child has chickenpox you'll find some useful remedies in the Babies and children section on pages 118–125. However, you may also want to check out the Skin chapter on pages 68–79 to find ways to help soothe the inflamed rash that accompanies the chickenpox virus. Alongside the remedies are plenty of recipes that you can create at home.

This book is designed to empower you to be able to take control of your own health using your kitchen and garden. You will also find instructions on how to create a healing herb garden and in each chapter a spotlight on one of my favourite herbal healers. I have chosen plants that are well known, easy to find and that I use regularly at home, such as nettles, rose, lavender and comfrey. In addition I have put together my suggestions for a herbal first aid kit (see page 17) that you can have on hand for emergencies, including my top recommendations for treatments to carry when out and about.

Plant knowledge

It is a good idea to familiarize yourself with what plants grow in your area.
Spend time in the garden with a notebook to record what you find. Make
drawings, press leaves and flowers between the pages and take notes. It
doesn't have to be scientific. Make notes about what you see and how you
interpret the plants around you. Ask questions – does it have large or
small leaves? What are they shaped like? Is it flowering now? Where is the
plant growing – in shade or full sun? Soon you will start to build up a good
knowledge of the plants growing in your backyard, then you can start to
learn about their healing properties. Don't expect this knowledge to come
all at once. I have been working with and learning about plants for over
15 years and there is still so much more to learn, but each season I gather
a bit more knowledge about what I can use to help heal my family.

Once you have studied the plants in your area, take your notebook further afield and observe the hedgerows around your home, local wasteland or park. Make notes on what is growing or flowering now, what is coming up and where you found it. Highlight plants to visit again in a couple of weeks time. For example, if you spot an elder covered with tiny white buds in mid-Spring, make a note to come back in a week and you'll be rewarded with plumes of frothy white flowers that can be harvested to make an excellent remedy for hayfever. Soon you will have built up knowledge of your local plants; you will possess an invaluable resource for when it comes to treating your body holistically. You can use your knowledge to create a map of natural healing remedies that are easily accessible in your area.

It will soon start to become second nature to brew up a batch of nettle tonic in early spring or to harvest a couple of handfuls of hawthorn berries in the autumn to make a hearty concoction of hawthorn brandy that can be used to treat heart conditions in the months ahead. For these and many more recipes, take a look inside.

Caution: herbs to avoid in pregnancy

Many herbs and herbal remedies can be used safely throughout pregnancy to offer natural relief from the various discomforts and ailments that may occur. However some herbs should be avoided. It is a good idea to consult a herbalist or get hold of a book that specifically deals with using herbs during pregnancy to help you identify those plants that are not safe for use at this special time.

Essential home remedy kit

To learn about natural remedies it is a good idea to build up a toolkit of home medicines that you can try out on yourself, your family and friends. I have listed some of the basic remedies that I like to have on hand here. Your family may have differing needs so you may want to add to this basic selection with natural medicines found in the specific ailments sections on pages 26–125.

It is helpful to have the remedies that you use frequently on hand, so that they are easily accessible when you need them. I have a shelf in a kitchen cupboard where I keep some of my remedies. Others, such as garlic, can be found in the vegetable basket or as herbs, growing in pots by the front door.

You might like to include a notebook in your kit. This can be useful for noting down what you have used, on what date, on whom and how effective it was at treating the problem. This will be a great source of information for your family when a similar problem occurs.

Tool kit basics

Garlic
A powerful treatment for a range of ailments. Use raw as a decongestant and to treat infection. I like to make it into a syrup with honey for chesty coughs and colds.

Lemon juice
Has antibacterial qualities and is very cleansing. Combined with honey, lemon juice makes a soothing treatment for colds and coughs.

Aloe vera
I have several pots of this succulent growing around the house. It can be used on burns, stings and irritated skin to give almost instant relief.

Cloves
Excellent for treating toothache as they act as an analgesic. Pop one in your mouth and chew on it until the pain subsides.

Ginger
Grated into boiling water to make a tea, this root will soothe respiratory and digestive problems. Combine with lemon juice and honey to make a powerful remedy for colds and coughs.

Honey
An effective treatment for burns, it can also be used to make a soothing drink for sore throats and colds.

Lavender oil
I like to always have a supply of this essential oil available. It can be used on bites and stings, cuts and wounds to help the skin to heal and also applied to the temples to soothe a headache.

Camomile
Whenever anyone in my family gets an eye infection I turn to camomile tea. I've even used it on our pet guinea pigs and cat. Allow the tea to cool and bathe the infected eye using organic cotton pads or a clean flannel.

Calendula

I keep this on hand as an ointment to treat sore, irritated skin and also just to use as a lip balm or moisturiser. I like to grow it in the herb beds for the beautiful sunshiny flowers, which can be used in a number of skincare preparations and also as a colourful addition to a salad.

Comfrey

An ointment made from this plant is useful for treating bruises and bites. I have a large pot of this magical plant growing by the front door.

Peppermint

Peppermint tea can be used to treat indigestion or headaches. Pick a handful and steep in boiling water for ten minutes. Strain and drink as it is, or sweeten with honey to taste.

Arnica

I use the homeopathic remedy and cream regularly so always have some available at home. It can be used in cases of (non-medical) shock and to treat bumps and bruises.

Rescue remedy

Every home should have a little bottle of this blend of five flower essences. It can be used to treat mild shock, trauma and injury. Take five drops on the tongue or dilute in a glass of water for younger children.

Your herbal first aid kit

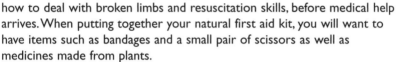

It is a good idea to put together a pack of remedies that can be used for first aid at home. There are many natural treatments that can easily be administered to treat the body in times of shock and distress. As well as having a good selection of remedies at home to treat emergencies, it might be worthwhile enrolling on a first aid course where you can learn the basics of administering first aid, such as how to deal with broken limbs and resuscitation skills, before medical help arrives. When putting together your natural first aid kit, you will want to have items such as bandages and a small pair of scissors as well as medicines made from plants.

You may want to make up a smaller kit for taking out and about. A portable kit that fits easily in a backpack is a good idea for holidays, walks and days out. Items that I would recommend for your portable first aid kit are marked with an asterisk.

Bites and stings

Stings are fairly common and easily dealt with using natural remedies. If an allergic reaction occurs seek the advice of a doctor.
Plantain can ease the pain and reduce swelling. Chew the leaf in your mouth and apply the masticated leaves as a poultice to the sting.
Lavender oil* can be applied directly to a sting.
Rescue remedy* If the person who has been stung is in distress, five drops taken on the tongue will work to calm the patient.
Aloe vera can be applied to the affected area. Split a leaf and spread the juice onto the skin.

* = recommended for your
portable first aid kit

Mild shock

Mild shock can be successfully treated with
natural remedies, however this condition
should not be confused with medical shock
which always requires medical attention.

Rescue remedy* to treat a patient who has experienced trauma.
Camomile tea can be calming for the nervous system. Brew a cup and
encourage the patient to take small sips while still warm.
Lavender oil* can be used to aleviate shock. Place a few drops onto a
handkerchief and inhale until the shock subsides.
Aconite, Arnica* and **Ignatia** are all homeopathic remedies that can be
used to treat shock and distress.

For cuts and wounds

If possible, raise the cut above the level of the heart (e.g. if the cut is on
the arm, lift the arm above the head). Apply direct pressure to the area
and continue until the flow of blood
stops, or in more serious cases
until medical help arrives.

Aloe vera can be applied to cuts
and grazes and will help skin to
heal and prevent infection.

Tea tree* or **Lavender oil*** are
used to clean wounds with a few
drops of each diluted in warm
water. This will also act as an
antiseptic.

Hypericum and **Arnica*** are
homeopathic remedies that can
be used to help the body to
heal.

Rescue remedy* can be
applied directly to a graze to
promote healing.

Comfrey ointment* can be
applied to inflamed cuts.

Comfrey ointment

▶ 500 g (1¼ lb) soft beeswax
▶ 60 g (2¼ oz) dried (or 150 g / 5 oz
fresh) comfrey leaves, finely chopped

1. Melt the beeswax in a glass bowl
over a pan of boiling water.
2. Add the comfrey leaves and
simmer, stirring continuously, for
about 1 hour.
3. Pour the mixture into a muslin bag.
Wearing rubber gloves, squeeze the
mixture through the bag into a jug.
4. Pour the ointment into a jar before
it sets. Place the lid on the jar,
without securing it.
5. When cool, tighten the lid and
store in a refrigerator for up to
3 months.

Burns and scalds

First pour cold liquid onto the burn or scald for at least 10 minutes, then use whichever of the following treatments you have available.
Aloe vera will cool the area and prevent infection. Split a leaf and gently apply the juice to the affected area.
Honey will help the skin to heal. Apply to the affected area.
Lavender oil* can be used neat on a burn to promote healing and prevent infection. Gently massage a few drops into the affected area.

Sunstroke

This is a type of heat exhaustion resulting from prolonged exposure to sun, often accompanied by headache, shivering, nausea and dizziness.
Rescue remedy* will help the patient to recover. Take five drops in a glass of water and sip slowly.

Food poisoning

Warm water mixed with the juice of half a lemon will help to cleanse the system.
Honey can be dissolved in a glass of warm water and sipped frequently to increase strength and boost the immune system.
Bio live yogurt can be eaten after the vomiting has subsided to help repopulate the stomach with beneficial bacteria.
Camomile tea can be calming and soothing for the digestive system.
A tonic can be made using herbs from the kitchen cupboard, which will help to cleanse the system.

* = recommended for portable first aid kit

Cleansing tonic

▶ 1 tsp black pepper
▶ 2 cloves garlic, crushed
▶ 1 tbsp cumin seeds
▶ pinch salt
▶ 600 ml (1 pint) water

1. Place the ingredients into a pan and boil until the liquid is reduced by half.
2. Drink twice a day to help cleanse the system and to treat diarrhoea.

Growing your own medicine

Herbs have been used by humans throughout history as medicines, perfumes, insect repellents and, of course, in food. In most cases, herbs are perennial and are tough wild plants which, when introduced to the luxurious conditions of a garden, will thrive. Planting your own medicine garden is a simple, pleasurable activity that will benefit you and your family for many years to come. It is a good idea to plant a small herb garden near the house that you can use as a medicine chest. Apothecary gardens have been grown for centuries full of the healing powers of plants.

Positioning your herb bed as close to the house as possible will make tending and harvesting easier. When planning an apothecary garden remember that not all herbs like full sun; divide the area into sun, partial shade and full shade and plant accordingly. I recommend selecting a circular plot and making a herb spiral.

Creating a herb spiral

A herb spiral is as simple as it sounds: a large spiral structure, typically measuring one and a half to two meters/yards wide diameter at the base, spiralling up to a height of around one meter, with a planting path running up it. A herb spiral of these proportions is big enough to accommodate at least all of the basic herbs included here, and a few slightly more exotic ones too.

There are many advantages of creating a herb spiral. First, by making use of both the vertical and the horizontal space, it allows you to make maximum use of a small growing area. This is particularly beneficial to those with little or no garden. The curved nature of the planting beds also increases the growing area available, compared to more traditional straight-edged gardens. Due to its design, the herb spiral offers a variety of different microclimates and aspects that are all easily accessible.

The benefits of this diversity of habitats are obvious – the gardener is able to plant a wide range of plants, all with differing needs and uses, in a very small area. Oil-rich herbs, such as rosemary, thyme and sage, can be grown on the dry and sunny top southerly side, whereas the moist and sheltered base on the northerly side is perfect for green foliage herbs such as mint, parsley and coriander. There is even the potential to create a small pond or bog area at the base of the spiral for plants such as watercress and watermint.

Virtually any building materials can be used to construct the herb spiral, as long as they're reasonably long-lived and not likely to rot away as untreated wood is liable to do. Anything from wooden stakes to large slates, bricks, stones, bottles stacked on their side, or even scrap tyres can be used to create the walls of the spiral. If you are building directly onto earth, it's advisable to mulch the area beforehand, to prevent weed problems whilst the herbs are establishing themselves. You can use anything water permeable, such as cardboard or old carpet. If you are building onto concrete, break it up to ensure adequate drainage. You can choose one of two methods of construction. The simplest and possibly less stable method, at least while the herbs are becoming established, is to pile the soil into a large heap and insert stones, slates, etc. to create a spiral shape. Because there is a danger of the soil washing away in rain or blowing away in wind before the plants are established, it is best to use pot-grown plants if you choose this method.

The second method is more permanent and more involved. First, stake out the spiral shape using sticks or bamboo. The base should be between one and a half to two metres/yards in diameter. Next, construct the walls using bricks or stones, starting from the outside and moving inwards. Add more layers, gradually increasing the height as you move into the centre. If you are using bricks and mortar, add the soil at the end. If you are using a 'dry stone' technique (just stacking the stones on top of one another), add the soil as you go to give more support and stability.

Try and use relatively weed-free soil. If soil or well-rotted compost is in short supply, you can try using a base layer of fresh manure or unrotted organic waste with a 10 cm (4 in) layer of soil on top, but be wary of the spiral settling as your base layer breaks down. You may need to add more soil at this stage if this is the case.

Some herbs may require different soil conditions from others, however most will do well in good soil or compost. With careful planning, you can provide the optimum conditions for each by, for example, adding sand to the soil for Mediterranean herbs such as rosemary.

To build a pond or bog at the base, first put down a layer of sand or old carpet to prevent stones or other sharp objects from puncturing the liner. Next, install a plastic liner and smooth a thin layer of mud around its surface to enable pond fauna and flora to establish quicker. Bury the edge of the lining under rocks and soil to prevent it from slipping. To build the bog area, use a perforated liner.

Herbs for your herb spiral

Calendula
This sunny annual has beautiful yellow/orange flowers that bloom from mid-spring to early summer. It is one of the most widely used and effective medicinal plants. The flowers are loaded with healing properties including essential oils, saponins, carotenoid and flavonoids. It can be used to heal wounds, reduce inflammations and treat bruises, burns and cuts. In skincare, it is used to treat acne, eczema, rosacea and irritated or inflamed skin.
Grow Sow seeds under cover in early spring – germination takes 5 to 14 days – or sow direct into soil on the southern side of the herb spiral in late spring when risk of frost has passed.
Harvest Pick flowers as soon as they open in early summer. Young leaves can be eaten in salads.
Uses Good for nappy rash and skin complaints including cuts, grazes, minor burns, wounds and fungal conditions. Sap from the stem has traditionally been used to treat warts, corns and calluses.

Lavender

A woody perennial shrub with purple/bluish flowers
that grow upwards on tall stems. It originated in
the Mediterranean but now grows all over
Europe and the US. The list of healing
benefits of the lavender plant seems
never ending – it is anti-inflammatory, antispasmodic and
antiseptic. Essential oil can be applied

direct to the skin to treat burns, bruising and aching or tense muscles. In
skincare the oil can be used to alleviate dry skin conditions, acne,
dermatitis and rosecea. It stimulates cell renewal and healing so is a useful
ingredient in many skincare preparations.

Grow Sow seeds under cover in spring. Germination takes around three
weeks. Take softwood cuttings in late spring. Once these take root they
can be planted up on the drier, southern side of the herb spiral.

Harvest Cut flowers in summer just as they open.

Uses Make a scented oil that can be used to relax and soothe tired
bodies and minds. Place sachets of dried lavender leaves and flowers in
wardrobes to deter moths or under pillows to aid sleep.

Rosemary

A hardy perennial evergreen with flower spikes of
tiny violet blooms starting in early spring to early
summer. Needle shaped green leaves.

Grow Sow under protection in early spring –
germination takes 7 to 14 days – or take cuttings of
new growth in summer after flowers have finished.
Pot-up when well rooted and plant out on the
southern banks of the herb spiral the following year.

Harvest Pick leaves throughout the year.

Uses As well as aiding memory retention and
recovery from long-term illness, this herb can make
a good insect repellent. Rub leaves into temples to
alleviate headaches. A hair rinse can be made from
the leaves.

Camomile

This hardy evergreen perennial produces large single white daisy-like flowers throughout the summer. Leaves are green and sweet-smelling.
Grow Start off in early spring under cover. Germination usually takes 2 to 3 weeks. Take cuttings or divide plants in the spring, to start new plants. They can then be planted-up on the eastern side of the herb spiral to catch the early morning sun.
Harvest Pick flowers as they open and dry them or use fresh.
Uses Due to the plant's sedative properties the dried flowers are used to treat insomnia, digestive disorders and travel sickness. A hair rinse can be made for fair hair. Tea made from the dried flowers can also be used to make a rinse for use in homemade baby wipes and as a treatment for irritated skin.

Borage

A pretty flowering hardy annual that originates from the Mediterranean. Also known as starflower this herb was traditionally given to Roman soldiers for courage and comfort. The plant has several culinary and medicinal uses. Blue star-shaped flowers bloom from early summer to the first frosts. The mild green leaves are bristly, oval and succulent.
Grow Sow seeds into pots in early spring under protection. Germination takes from 5 to 14 days. When ready to plant out, position on the western side of the slopes of the herb spiral.
Harvest Pick fresh flowers just as they begin to open fully. You can preserve them in ice cubes. The leaves taste good in soups and salads.
Uses A facial steam for dry sensitive skin can be made with borage leaves as well as the flowers.

Wild strawberry

A hardy perennial with small white flowers that give way to
tiny red fruit in the summer months. Leaves are also edible.
Grow Pick fruit, dry them on cloth and then rub off seeds into a
tray of moist compost in the autumn. Germination takes
6 to 10 weeks. Cover with a plastic bag to protect and keep
warm. Plant out on the western side of the spiral when large
enough to handle. The mature plants produce runners that
can be trained into pots to make new plants. Place a pot full
of compost under the green shoot at the end of the runner.
Cut away from the main plant once rooted.
Harvest Pick ripe fruit from summer through to early autumn.
Uses Can be made into a treatment to prevent discolouration
of teeth.

Other possibilities for the herb spiral

Sweet violet This creeping evergreen perennial grows to approximately
15 cm (6 in). Both the leaves and flowers are tasty in winter salads. It can
be used as a gentle expectorant and is excellent for breast health. Can be
made into a poultice to treat breast lumps and mastitis.

Sorrel This native perennial will reach a mature size of 60 cm (24 in)
high and 30 cm (11¾ in) wide. It is very tolerant of a range of conditions,
and is easily grown. Delicious when eaten in salads and a good source
of nutrients.

Lemon balm At maturity, this herb is 70 cm (27½ in) tall and 40 cm
(16 in) wide. It is very tolerant of a range of conditions and will succeed
in light shade. The lemon-flavoured leaves can be used to make a refreshing
tea that is uplifting and often used in treatment of depression or anxiety.

Wild garlic Grows well in wet soils and will reach a height of up to
30 cm (11¾ in). The garlic-flavoured leaves are available in late winter/early
spring and can be used in place of garlic in cooking.

Treating ailments

The following pages include many common ailments, illnesses and medical conditions that can be successfully treated or soothed using natural remedies. The ailments are grouped by bodily systems but you may find that you need to look in more than one section to find the selection of treatments that will work for you.

Mind and emotions

Mentally, we are all affected by the situations that surround us. Sometimes this can become overwhelming and we can suffer from stress. If you regularly suffer from insomnia, depression, anxiety, feeling foggy-headed, dizziness, nausea, feeling drained of energy, or suffer from persistent bacterial and viral infections, it's time to take action. These symptoms of exhaustion are now widespread and can, at worst, lead to physical collapse.

Diet and physical exercise are both vital for mental health. We really are what we eat. Caffeine, sugar and fats can play havoc on our bodies and affect our well-being, so think carefully about what you're eating. If you are having persistent problems then a food sensitivity test might be a good idea, and an experienced nutritionist may be able to help. You may find that some foods are not being processed effectively, which can cause you to feel both mentally and physically out of balance. Wheat, yeast, dairy and sugar are the usual culprits. Try eliminating these from your diet one at a time over the course of a week to check how your body reacts to these foods. Be sure to include plenty of fresh greens, nuts, seeds and protein to help keep your body healthy whilst eliminating toxins.

Introducing regular, gentle exercise is another important step towards a happier, healthier mind. Aerobic exercise releases feel-good hormones – known as endorphins – which leave you feeling much brighter after a burst of activity. Be aware that the information we feed ourselves with affects us too – if you can, avoid the newspaper and news programmes full of doom and gloom about the state of the world. Choose to read something inspirational or watch an uplifting film instead.

Meditation can be very beneficial in ensuring good mental health and you may find that regular practice helps to improve concentration and memory. Your general mood should lift, sleep will be deeper and more regular and problems will seem less insurmountable. Bach Flower Remedies have been specially formulated to treat emotional disorders. The blend of five flower essences, Rescue Remedy is a good place to start as it can be used to treat so many differing conditions. Use it when you are feeling low or anxious.

Addiction

A dependence on a substance such as alcohol or nicotine. Physical withdrawal symptoms can include craving, mood swings and depression. Try using anti-depressant oils such as camomile, ylang ylang and clary sage. A few drops of each can be added to a carrier oil such as organic sweet almond oil. Use this to massage into your arms, chest and legs. It can also be added to a warm bath for an uplifting treat. Also, you might like to add a few drops of clary sage to your cuffs and collar when getting dressed to help you carry the scent with you and allow you to feel the effects all day long. Oats are a useful remedy for helping you to strengthen your willpower when letting something go from your life. They also have a calming effect on the mind. Make oat water (see page 30) and drink three times a day.

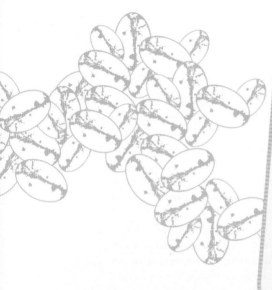

Oat water

Mentally this is good for strengthening willpower, and physically it can be used to treat the symptoms of diarrhoea and cystitis.

▶ 1 tbsp oats
▶ 1 cup of water

1. Combine the oats and water in a bowl, stir and leave to infuse for 20 minutes.
2. Stir again and strain the mixture through a muslin cloth.
3. Drink the resulting the liquid. The muslin cloth containing the oats can be tied and used as a bath bag to soothe the skin and also to calm the mind and aid more restful sleep.

Anxiety

A state of fear or apprehension that can become constant. It is associated with depression and causes symptoms such as sweaty palms, rapid pulse, breathlessness, headaches and loss of appetite. Oat can be used as a gentle nerve tonic. Eat porridge for breakfast to benefit from their effects. Also try oat water (above). This tonic can be taken three times a day to help you get over challenging times. Use Rescue Remedy during panic attacks. Place a few drops on the tongue or rub into the pulse points.

Depression

Often triggered by a stressful life event, depression is a feeling of despondency and unhappiness that lasts for a long time. Some women experience this after childbirth, when it is known as Post Natal Depression. Borage (also known as starflower) is recognised for its uplifting properties. A tincture can be made from the bright blue flowers.

Borage tincture

This tincture can help to lift the spirits when everything seems hopeless.

▶ A handful of borage flowers
▶ 200 ml (7 fl oz) alcohol, such as organic vodka or brandy
▶ 100 ml (3½ fl oz) water

1. Place the borage flowers in a large glass jar with a well-fitting lid.
2. Cover with the alcohol and water.
3. Replace the lid and leave to infuse for two weeks, gently shaking from time to time.
4. Strain the mixture though a muslin cloth, retaining the liquid. Bottle the tincture and store.
5. To drink, add 1 tsp to a glass of water.

Nurturing tea

Try this calming, nurturing tea when you are feeling low.

▶ Motherwort
▶ Lemon Balm

1. Pick equal amounts of Motherwort and Lemon Balm. Spread on a baking tray and leave in a warm, dry place for a week.
2. Once dried, crumble into a glass jar and store.
3. To drink, place 2 tsp of the dried herbs into a cup. Fill with boiling water and leave to infuse for ten minutes. Strain and drink.

Insomnia

This refers to the inability to sleep or disturbance of sleep patterns. Can be caused by emotional stress, worry and exhaustion. Excess caffeine, rich food and alcohol can also play a part in disturbed sleep patterns. There are plenty of suggestions for helping the mind to rest before sleep but one of the most effective is to keep a notepad by the bed and to jot down whatever is occupying the mind before sleep. I find that this can act as a sort of internal brain cleanse; getting everything out and onto paper so

Herbal bath bag

Make this herbal bath bag for a soak just before bed, which should help you get a good night's rest.

▶ 1 tbsp each of dried camomile flowers, dried lavender flowers and oats

1. Take a 30 cm (11¾ in) square of muslin and lay it out flat.
2. Place the dried flowers and oats in the centre of the muslin square. Gather up the corners and tie with string to secure.
3. Place in a warm bath and relax.

that my mind is ready to let go and go to sleep. A short yoga practice using calming poses such as shoulder stand followed by a relaxation listening to Yoga Nidra can also help to promote restful sleep. Yoga Nidra is known as the yogic sleep and is deeply relaxing to the mind and body. It is a great way to settle before drifting off at night. You can also use the power of mustard and take a hot footbath before bed to help calm the mind (see recipe on page 62). The mustard draws blood away from the head, aiding relaxation.

Memory loss

Also known as amnesia, this is a partial or complete memory loss, caused by a physical or mental disease or sometimes from a physical trauma such as a blow to the head. While anyone experiencing memory loss should consult a medical professional, rosemary can help to refresh the memory in minor cases when use in cooking or make a herbal tea. Place a small handful of chopped rosemary into a cup, cover with boiling water, leave to infuse for ten minutes. Strain and then drink. Enjoy as needed (up to three cups) throughout the day.

Obsessive compulsive disorder

An obsession to perform a certain ritual. This can be something as simple as repeated hand washing or repeated checking that the windows are shut at night, for example. It usually starts after a stressful life event, and minor obsessions and compulsions are said to affect 15 per cent of the population. camomile is a good herb to help calm the mind, release tension and encourage a letting go of behavioural patterns. Use as a tea and drink as often as needed throughout the day. Burn the essential oil of camomile in an oil burner along with marjoram, both of which are helpful in encouraging you to find balance. You can also add a few drops of each to a warm relaxing bath.

Phobias

This is a fear of something that can cause disruption to everyday living. Agoraphobia (fear of open spaces) and acrophobia (fear of heights) are some of the more common phobias, but they can range from fear of another person or an object to any number of experiences or situations. It is said that 10 per cent of the population have a phobia of one kind or another. The flower essences created by Dr. Bach were developed to help people deal with emotional problems and there are a number of remedies that can help with phobias. Rescue Remedy for example can be used to treat causes of mild to severe panic – place five drops on the tongue, or apply to pulse points on the wrist and behind the ears.

Aromatherapy can be very beneficial in the treatment of phobias. A blend of essential oils such as bergamot, lavender, melissa and ylang ylang can be calming and rebalancing to the nervous system when in a state of distress. Add a few drops of each to a carrier oil to make up a bath blend. It will have a slight sedative effect.

Fear diffuser

This can be spritzed as often as necessary during challenging times.

▶ A few drops of bergamot, lavender, melissa and ylang ylang essential oils
▶ Spring water

1. Take a small spray top bottle and add a few drops each essential oil.
2. Top up with spring water.
3. Spritz over the face (close your eyes) and wrists as needed.

Stress

This is a growing disorder in our modern world. Many factors can affect our mental health, such as inadequate diet, environment, noise pollution and financial strains. This mental discomfort has a knock-on effect on the body, encouraging a rapid production of hormones, which can cause increased breathing and heart rate, leading to nausea and tense muscles. As soon as the stressful situation is resolved the body returns to normal. If the situation continues, energy levels dwindle and exhaustion sets in. Fortunately there are many natural treatments for this common disorder. The first and most obvious is to take a good look at your life and address the common triggers for stress. Are you putting in longer and longer hours at work? Do you feel that your responsibilities at home are too great with children to care for, a house to keep tidy and a household to run? Make a list of things that stress you out – school run, cooking for the family, monthly reports at work, for example. Acknowledging these stressful situations is the first step in dealing with them. Once you have a list of stressful things in your life take the first item on your list and brainstorm who or what could support you. Perhaps your neighbour could take the children to school and you could collect them? Maybe you could have a picnic supper at the weekends, or a takeaway night, or perhaps someone else in your household could take over the cooking for a while. The monthly reports might be a task that could be completed by a colleague. Stick this list up in a prominent place and start to action the alternatives. There are also a number of natural remedies that can support you in this process.

Starting the day with a bowl of porridge helps to strengthen the system and gives you a clearer and more positive outlook. Bathe with a few drops of essential oils of camomile, geranium, lavender, neroli and rose. Add a few drops of each (or whichever you have to hand) to warm running water and sink in for a relaxing, uplifting experience that can help to wash your troubles away.

Ten tips to de-stress

Here are some ideas for when the going gets tough. Always try to remember that tomorrow is another day. If all else fails, get an early night and wake up with a fresh take on life.

1. Wake up early in the morning to enjoy half an hour quiet time on your own. This will allow you time to collect your thoughts and energise yourself for the day ahead.

2. Go for a bracing walk. Exercise releases serotonin, the happy hormone, so you start to feel better as soon as you get into your stride.

3. Arrange a night in with your partner. Using some sensual essential oils, give each other a massage.

4. Breathe properly. Many of us use only a tenth of our lung capacity. Imagine how good we would feel if we learn to use half or more? Breath work can teach us how to use more of our lungs' full potential.

5. Run a warm bath, surround it with candles, climb in and relax.

6. Laugh. Phone a friend who makes you laugh or rent a funny movie.

7. Retreat to a quite place such as a favourite armchair and enjoy a good book.

8. Take your family out for the day. Getting away from the house and the daily routine of chores does everyone the world of good once in a while.

9. Take an evening course in something you feel passionate about.

10. If all hell is breaking loose and you feel your stress levels rising, walk into another room and count slowly to ten before returning to salvage the situation.

Rose

The rose is an uplifting and sensual plant. Lovers have recognized this beautiful perfumed flower since ancient times – Cleopatra was said to have strewn the floor with rose petals when she invited Mark Anthony into her boudoir. Today, couples can use roses to encourage love and communication. Try bathing together in a bathtub filled with rose petals and a few drops of rose essential oil. Or make your own massage blend using sweet almond oil as a base with 4 drops each of rose and ylang ylang. Rose petals make an alluring addition to a warm bath and a handful thrown under running water can actually help to alleviate rheumatic pains. Sore, tired eyes can be soothed using an infusion, made by steeping a few rose petals in hot water. Strain before use and use several times a day until symptoms have cleared up.

Many natural toiletries use the power and scent of rose and rose oil is often used as a perfume. It is one of the world's most expensive commodities, weight by weight worth more than gold. Aromatherapists value it for its uplifting and soothing properties, especially for nervous tension. When the blooms have faded and the petals fallen away, the plant bears a fruit called a hip, containing seeds, which are rich in Vitamin C. They also contain B vitamins and a high amount of carotene. During the Second World War, due to a shortage of fruit and vegetables, children were encouraged to pick rose hips on their way to school so that they could be boiled up to make a nutritive syrup, which was issued as a dietary supplement.

Rosehips are excellent for the skin, can help to prevent infection and are also a known blood purifier. The Chinese use rosehip tea to relieve stomachache and to regulate vital energy. This tea can also be blended with a pinch of cloves and cinnamon to stimulate and restore the system. It is best to avoid drinking this tea late at night as rosehips stimulate the adrenal glands.

In cooking, rose petals have been used for centuries to add elegance as well as for added nutrition. Try tossing a few petals into a fruit salad, or as a cake decoration. Rosehips can be used to make a fine hedgerow wine, jams, jellies, syrups, tarts, breads and in many other forms of baking. They impart a good colour and a subtle sweetness to many dishes.

To harness the healing powers of the rosehip as the Chinese do, without the use of a great deal of sugar that is needed to produce a syrup, try making rosehip tea. Use one teaspoon of crushed rose hips to one cup of water. Boil for 20 minutes and then sieve through muslin to remove the irritating hairs on the fruits. Four cups of this tea can be taken daily to restore the system.

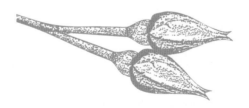

Nervous system

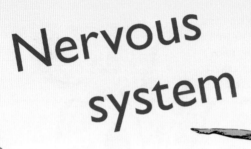

A little stress can be healthy for the heart and mind. However, it is easy for us to tip over the edge into anxiety, panic and even depression. Stress affects the whole person, physically, mentally and emotionally. This is why holistic therapies are such a powerful weapon against the effects of stress as they work on all levels to try and bring you back into balance, body, mind and spirit.

Multiple sclerosis

A chronic disease of the nervous system that affects the sheaths of the nerves, which become inflamed, leading to gradual loss of nerve function. The disease is characterised by its cycle of remission and relapse. Practicing yoga can help prevent further deterioration of the disorder as it improves flexibility of the limbs and prevents stiffness. Regular massage of the joints is helpful, as is water therapy. At home, try hot mineral baths with Epsom salts, alternating between hot and cold showers to help stimulate the nerves twice a day. Add raw dairy and cultured products to the diet such as raw unsalted butter (preferably organic and from grass-fed cows), homemade cottage cheese and unfiltered honey. Increase intake of gamma-linoleic acid found in safflower and evening primrose oil. Rescue Remedy can be used to help ease the symptoms and relieve anxiety.

Stroke

A stroke is a condition where a blood clot or ruptured artery or blood vessel interrupts blood flow to an area of the brain. A lack of oxygen and glucose flowing to the brain causes damage, often resulting in impaired speech, movement and memory. Smaller strokes may result in minor problems, such as weakness in an arm or leg. Larger strokes may lead to paralysis. Many stroke patients are left with weakness on one side of the body, difficulty speaking, incontinence and bladder problems. Gently massage the body daily especially the paralyzed muscles. Use a carrier oil such as organic sweet almond oil with a few drops of rosemary essential oil.

> **Yarrow or rosemary tea**
>
> Yarrow and rosemary can both help to improve circulation.
>
> ▶ A handful of yarrow leaves or three small sprigs of rosemary
>
> 1. Place the yarrow or rosemary in a cup and add boiling water.
> 2. Place a plate over the top and leave to infuse for ten minutes.
> 3. Strain and drink up to three cups daily.

Parkinson's disease

A serious chronic disease of the nervous system causing continuous tremors or shaking and stiffness of the neck. Oats are calming and strengthening to the nervous system. You can make your own nerve tonic to drink regularly throughout the day.

> **Nerve tonic**
>
> ▶ 1 tbsp oats
> ▶ 300 ml (½ pint) water
>
> 1. Place the oats and water in a saucepan.
> 2. Bring to the boil and simmer for five minutes.
> 3. Strain and drink as needed.

Epilepsy

A serious disease of the central nervous system, this chronic condition presents as repeated fits or attacks of unconsciousness with often violent shivers. Attacks generally reduce with age, but the uncertainty in the time of attack is one major problem. Avoid physical and mental stress. Take a warm Epsom salts bath once a day and take Rescue Remedy as you feel an attack coming on.

Shingles

A painful disease caused by the herpes zoster virus (chickenpox). Symptoms can include sensitivity in the affected area, high fever, sickness and a painful rash of small blisters. Use crushed plantain leaves to soothe neuralgic pains and rash. Crush the leaves and apply to the affected area. Re-apply as often as needed. Bathe the infected area with diluted tincture of calendula (see page 98), plantain or St. John's Wort. Dilute 1 part to 10 parts water, soak a cloth and apply a cold compress to the affected area.

Plantain tincture

▶ A large handful of plantain leaves
▶ 200 ml (7 fl oz) alcohol such as organic vodka
▶ 100 ml (3½ fl oz) water

1. Place the plantain leaves in a large glass jar and cover with the alcohol and water.
2. Put on the lid and leave for two weeks, shaking occasionally.
3. Strain the liquid through a sieve with a muslin cloth over it.
4. Pour the liquid into a dark glass bottle and store for up to a year.

Migraine

A severe headache that generally occurs on one side of the head, it is associated with disorders of digestion, liver and vision. Migraines usually occur when a person is under great mental tension. The pain lasts around 3 days, and may be accompanied by nausea and vomiting. Eye disturbances can occur such as intolerance of light, blurred vision, black spots or zigzag line that appear before the eyes, or partly blank vision. The headache is usually accompanied by weakness in an arm or leg and tingly and numb feeling. Patients tend to be compulsive workers with overworked and continuously stressed head and neck muscles. Apply a cold compress to the head and face. Add 2 drops of lavender oil to a bowl of cool water. Soak a cloth in the water, wring out and apply to the temples. Feverfew is a plant that can be used to treat migraine. Eat two small leaves with food.

Headache

A headache indicates that something is wrong somewhere in the body. Pain arises from irritation to the nerve endings in the shoulder, neck and scalp-muscles and in smooth muscles encircling the blood vessels. A ginger root footbath can help to ease the pain and warm the body. Fill a large bowl with warm water and add 2 inches of grated ginger root. Place your feet into the bowl and relax for 15 minutes. A mustard footbath can also be helpful (see page 62). Drink peppermint tea to calm and soothe the system and help to clear a tension headache. Massage a drop or two of lavender oil into your temples or the pulse points on the wrist. Alternatively, apply a few drops to a handkerchief and inhale regularly to reduce pain. Take a soothing warm bath; swirl in a few drops each of camomile, lavender and ylang ylang essential oil.

Neuralgia

Describes any pain that originates in the nerve. The pain may be intermittent or continuous. St. John's Wort is a traditional herbal remedy for nerve damage. Use the oil to gently massage the body.

St. John's wort oil

This oil can be used for massage to help heal nerve damage. It is also useful for treating skin complaints such as cold sores.

▶ A handful of flowering tops from the St. John's Wort plant
▶ 200 ml (7 fl oz) sunflower oil

1. Place the flowering tops in a pestle with a little of the the oil.
2. Pound together until you have a mash and put the mashed flowers into a large glass jar. Cover with more oil.
3. Shake well and leave in direct sunlight for 21 days. The oil will turn red when it is ready for use.

Rosemary

Rosemary is a multi-purpose herb – its leaves, flowers and essential oil can be used in a variety of ways including culinary, medicinal and in aromatherapy. It is a hardy shrubby perennial bush that grows up to 1.5 metres (1½ yards) high with green/grey needle-shaped evergreen leaves and pale blue/lilac flowers that attracts bees. It originates from Asia, but is now cultivated widely in many herb gardens in the West. Growing rosemary is relatively easy. Depending on your climate, rosemary can be planted in the garden as a border plant or single ornamental. It likes sun and good drainage, and does very well in hot or dry climates. It will tolerate freezing temperatures for a short time if it's protected from cold winds. During long, cold winters, cultivate in a pot that can be brought inside and left in a sunny window or greenhouse. Rosemary grows well in most soils, but thrives as a more fragrant plant in a more alkaline soil; so add ground eggshells or wood ash if your soil tends to the acidic side.

The name is derived from the Latin *Rosmarinus* or 'sea dew', as it loves water. The Egyptians, Hebrews, Greeks and Romans considered the herb to be sacred, and even in the Middle Ages it was used to ward off evil spirits and used as a protection against the plague. Rosemary was an essential part of the apothecary's repertoire during the Renaissance and

the French regarded it as a miraculous cure-all. Because rosemary was easily harvested from the wild it was used as an incense by the poor as a substitute for expensive frankincense or myrrh-based incense, in ancient Greece and Rome. When a twig of rosemary is burned it is said to rid space of negativity because of its cleansing vibrations. It was burnt at shrines in Ancient Greece to drive away evil spirits and illnesses.

Hippocrates, Galen and Dioscorides all prescribed rosemary for liver problems. Rosemary is an astringent, restorative herb that is excellent for muscle aches and strains and rheumatism. It increases the rate of perspiration while stimulating the liver and gall bladder. It improves digestion and circulation and has antibacterial, antifungal, antiviral, analgesic, anti-depressant and anti-inflammatory properties. It is an outstanding free radical scavenger and therefore has amazing antioxidant properties. It has a tightening, stimulating effect on the skin and is a wonderful treatment for the hair and scalp.

Rosemary essential oil is extracted from the fresh flowering tops by steam distillation and has a clear, powerful and refreshing herbal smell. It can be used in vaporizers and oil burners, in the bath or in a carrier oil for massage directly onto the skin. It has a highly stimulating action and because of this it may not be suitable for people with epilepsy or high blood pressure and should also not be used during pregnancy. It has a pronounced stimulating effect on the brain and central nervous system and is great for clearing the mind, improving memory and mental awareness.

The diuretic properties of rosemary oil are useful for reducing water retention caused by premenstrual tension and menstruation, and also for obesity and cellulite. It is also effective for asthma, bronchitis, catarrh, sinus problems and whooping cough. On the skin, it helps to ease congestion, puffiness and swelling and can also be used for acne, dermatitis and eczema.

Rosemary is a great thirst quencher and adding rosemary to your tea creates a unique flavour that is good for a pick-me-up. Pick a 10 cm (4 in) sprig, wash it, add to your teapot and steep for two to three minutes. The tea can be served with or without milk. Adding rosemary to marinades adds a refreshing, uplifting flavour. Add two teaspoons of crushed rosemary leaves to every two tablespoons of olive oil. Throw in a dash of tamari sauce and brush over butternut squash, mushrooms or potatoes and leave to marinade before baking or barbecuing. The flowers can also be added to salads.

Digestive system

Did you know that 70 per cent of your immune system lives in the gut? Were you aware that stomach acid, far from being a negative element, is a protective barrier, killing harmful bacteria? And did you realize that it's not just food, but lifestyle as well that helps you maintain a healthy acid/alkaline balance so that you can process your food efficiently for maximum wellbeing? Taking care of your digestive system means ensuring that you eat regular meals, rather than skipping meals or just having a coffee in the morning for breakfast. Try eating smaller meals more regularly, eating earlier in the evening, and not drinking too much water with meals, as this can dilute the gastric juices. Avoid rich, fatty food that is challenging for your digestive system to cope with, and also take care with things like fizzy drinks, which can be very acidic and irritating to the stomach lining.

Relaxation should be an important part of your eating routine. Don't eat while stressed. The digestion can be often 'turned off' by the fight or flight stress response. It is better to wait until you are calm so that the body is in a better state to receive food. Eating at a table with friends and family is a far healthier way for the body to receive nutrients than slumped in front of the TV.

Stomach acid is a necessary part of digestion, though it is often seen as a bad thing, to be controlled by antacids or acid blocking drugs. In fact many nutritionists see clients that have the opposite problem, they have too little stomach acid, which can also cause problems with indigestion. Herbs are excellent at healing stomach

complaints. They can help balance excess acid, soothe inflamed mucous membranes, and protect against the damage caused by many orthodox medications.

Stomach ulcers are becoming very common in younger, seemingly fit and healthy individuals. Stress, caffeine, overeating, erratic eating patterns, bad diet and not drinking enough water all lead to heat in the stomach causing ulceration. Traditional Chinese medicine calls this 'Stomach fire' as it literally feels like the stomach is on fire, with burning sensations, bleeding gums, constant hunger, bad breath and sluggish bowels. If these symptoms appear, even in a mild form, action must be taken. Spicy and fried foods, red meat, alcohol, citrus fruit, tomatoes, caffeine and tobacco will aggravate and make it very difficult for the stomach lining to heal. There are many alternative ways of dealing with stomach-related imbalances.

The liver is another important organ in the digestive system; it governs the digestive process and is responsible for regulating, cleaning and storing the blood in the body. It is our largest organ and is filled with blood. The better condition our liver is in, the better it can ensure that the blood that circulates around our bodies nourishes our muscles and keeps them supple and pain free. The liver makes bile to emulsify fats for digestion, makes and breaks down hormones, including cholesterol and oestrogens, and regulates blood sugar levels. One of its most important roles is detoxification. The liver manufactures 13,000 chemicals and has 2,000 enzyme systems critical to the smooth operation of our bodies and minds. Nearly all vitamins and minerals that we need are enzymatically processed by the liver before we can use them.

Some of the symptoms of liver problems are poor digestion, abdominal bloating, nausea after fatty foods, unstable blood sugar levels, waking with bad breath and/or coated tongue, intolerance to greasy/fatty foods, constipation, fatigue and sleepiness after eating, yellow whites of eyes, yellowish colour of skin, lowered tolerance to alcohol, and excessive body heat.

If you suspect an imbalance in your liver look out for a dip in energy in the late afternoon which leads to a craving for chocolate or something sweet, waking in the early hours of the morning and being unable to drop back off to sleep because of an over-active mind, unusual irritability over issues which do not generally cause such a reaction, or skin and digestive problems.

Fortunately there are a number of natural remedies that can be used to treat disorders of the digestive system. Find out how to improve your digestion using herbs such as fennel and dill, treat stomachache with rosehip tea and get things moving again in cases of constipation.

Nausea and vomiting

Symptom of many disorders including migraine, food poisoning and gastroenteritis. Stress and anxiety can cause feelings of nausea without vomiting. Ginger tea can be drunk to warm and ease stomach pain, especially when travelling causes nausea. Also useful in cases of morning sickness during pregnancy. Grate half a thumb-sized knob of fresh root of ginger into a cup and cover with boiling water. Allow to steep, strain and enjoy whilst still warm. Rescue remedy can be used and it will help calm the mind and soothe the body. Take five drops in a glass of water as needed.

Gastroenteritis

Acute inflammation of the stomach caused by bacteria or a virus. Fever usually accompanies with diarrhoea and abdominal pain. A teaspoon of honey taken every few hours will act as a natural antibiotic and is anti-inflammatory. It will also keep the body's strength up at a challenging time. Massage essential oil of roman chamomile into the abdomen area to ease discomfort. Take a tablespoon of live yoghurt three times a day when the symptoms start to ease, in order to repopulate the gut with healthy flora.

Stomach ache

The Chinese make a tea from rosehips
to alleviate stomach aches. This tea
also helps to regulate vital energy as it
stimulates the adrenal glands – avoid
late at night for this reason. To harness
the healing powers of the rosehip
without the use of a great deal of sugar
needed to produce a syrup, try making
rosehip tea.

Rosehip tea

1. Use one teaspoon of crushed rose
hips to one cup of water.
2. Boil for 20 minutes and then sieve
through muslin to remove the
irritating hairs on the fruits.
3. Four cups of this tea can be taken
daily to restore the system.

Indigestion and heartburn

This can cause discomfort in the
abdomen, often after eating rich food
or eating too quickly. Drink peppermint
tea to soothe the stomach and aid
digestion. You can also rub essential oil
of peppermint into the stomach to ease
discomfort. Fennel seeds eaten after a
meal can help the stomach to digest rich
foods. Make an infusion of dill to reduce
pains from trapped gas. Drink fresh cucumber juice
or eat a cucumber to reduce the effects of heartburn
or acid reflex.

Dill infusion

1. Pick a handful of dill and place in a
cup. Cover with boiling water and
place a plate over the top.
2. Leave to infuse for ten minutes.
3. Strain and drink whilst still warm.

Travel sickness

Sensitivity to motion when travelling can cause feelings of nausea
and also sickness. Take a flask of chamomile, peppermint or fennel
tea with you to sip throughout the journey. Chew fresh peppermint
leaves to settle the stomach.

Constipation

Painful or irregular bowel
movements caused by compacted
matter in the colon. Massage
rosemary or fennel oil into the
abdomen in a clockwise direction
to follow the movement of the
colon. Certain herbs have a laxative
effect and should be used with care but can help relieve
the body. Licorice is one such herb, which can be made into an infusion
and drunk as needed, up to three cups per day.

> **Liquorice infusion**
> 1. Place a stick of liquorice, broken into pieces, into a cup. Cover with boiling water and place a plate on top.
> 2. Leave to infuse for 10 minutes.
> 3. Strain through a tea strainer and drink as required.

Diarrhoea

Loose runny stools are the result of
many illnesses. Can also be caused
by stress or anxiety. Oats are a
soothing, binding food that can aid
gut health. Make some oat water
(see page 30) and drink three
times a day. Carrot juice is a
traditional remedy for diarrhoea,
especially for babies. You can also make a
carrot soup to soothe the bowel.

> **Carrot juice**
> 1. Juice 3 carrots in a juicer.
> 2. Pour into a glass and drink immediately.
> 3. Drink three times a day whilst symptoms persist.

Irritable bowel syndrome

A common disorder with abdominal pain
and diarrhoea alternating with constipation. Drink soothing
herbal teas of peppermint and chamomile, which all have anti-spasmodic
properties. Massage roman chamomile essential oil into the abdomen.

Flatulence

An excessive amount of gas in the body, often caused by eating foods that disagree with the digestive system or eating too quickly. Eat celery seeds to reduce flatulence. Make a dill infusion (see page 47) to ease any discomfort.

Hepatitis

Hepatitis means inflammation (itis) of the liver (hepar) – an irritation or swelling of the liver cells. There are many causes of hepatitis, including viral infections. Most of us will have heard of types A, B and C, but the variations also includes auto-immune hepatitis, fatty liver hepatitis, alcoholic hepatitis and toxin induced hepatitis. It is estimated that around 250 million people globally are affected by hepatitis C. Moreover, an estimated 400 million people are chronic carriers of hepatitis B. Liver tonics, such as milk thistle, dandelion and nettle, can be taken daily to help healing. Massage chamomile or grapefruit essential oils into the abdomen or take a warm bath with a few drops of either added.

Crohn's disease

Inflammation of the bowel, which can cause lower abdominal pain, anaemia and appetite and weight loss. Add a few drops of lavender oil to a warm bath to help you relax. Rub a few drops of chamomile essential oil into the abdomen to soothe pain. Drink an infusion of peppermint to soothe and protect the gut lining from irritation.

Peppermint infusion

This infusion can also help to ease the symptoms of travel sickness. Make the infusion in a flask and drink as required on your journey.

1. Pick a handful of peppermint leaves and place in a cup. Cover with boiling water and place a plate on top.
2. Leave to infuse for 10 minutes.
3. Strain through a tea strainer and drink as required.

Dandelion

The dandelion (*taraxacum officinale*) is thought have got its name due to the shape of its leaves, the wide teeth likened to lion's teeth (hence *dent-de-lion* in Old French). The plant is considered a weed by many but actually has high nutritive benefits and health boosting properties. The bane of many gardeners around the world, as fast as you pull them up, they sprout back and their taproot grows deep and strong.

This European plant was originally introduced to other continents to provide food for honeybees. Eighty-five different species of insects feast on its pollen and the seeds are enjoyed by songbirds. The plant is easily recognized, both in the spring and summer with its vibrant yellow ray flowers and in late summer when the seed head appears. The seed head can develop overnight and is composed of hundreds of tiny parachuted seeds, ready to spread far and wide into the wind to pollinate the plant.

When broken, the stem and the root exude a milky, sticky sap that can supposedly remove warts, pimples and sores. It can also be applied to bee stings and blisters to soothe and calm the inflammation. Despite the concept that dandelion is a bitter plant, the young leaves can be enjoyed raw in salads and other dishes. Today our palate is conditioned to prefer sweet or overly salty foods and to dislike bitter flavours but in earlier times dandelions were enjoyed regularly. Once you acquire a taste for them they can enhance a salad, adding a depth to its flavour. Harvest in early spring before the flowers grow. They can also be harvested

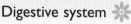

again in late autumn. Avoid any plants that might have been contaminated by herbicides or pesticides. Sautéed or steamed, dandelions have a much gentler flavour and can be added to soups, stews and breads.

Dandelion leaves are one of the most nutritious greens available to us. They have a greater concentration of beta-carotene than carrots, are very rich in iron and calcium and packed with vitamins and minerals. The flowers have traditionally been used to make wine. If you would like to try this, harvest the flowers in mid-spring, remove all green parts and find a recipe on the internet or in a wild food cookbook. The flowers can also brighten up a spring salad, or you can coat them in batter and fry lightly to make golden fritters.

The taproot can be eaten all year round and, although not as tasty as some other wild root vegetables, can be a useful ingredient to bulk out a potato and leek (or other spring vegetable) soup. A beer that acts as a blood purifier and tonic is made in Northern England by combining dandelion roots with burdock. A decoction of the taproot is believed to strengthen the body's whole system, especially the liver and gallbladder. Hence it is often used as part of an herbal spring clean for the body. A daily cup of tea made by steeping the leaves in boiling water can help people who are rundown, as it is so rich in vitamins and minerals. It is an excellent digestive aid. This strong tea can also be added to bathwater to soothe inflamed skin and eczema.

During the First World War when natural rubber supplies were cut off, Henry Ford experimented with latex made from dandelions as an alternative. He succeeded in making a high quality product but had problems in sourcing the quantities that he needed and the research was abandoned at the end of the war. In Druid lore, to dream of a dandelion is a symbol of difficult times ahead, a period of change and challenge that can have beneficial effect on the dreamer. Children use the seed heads as clocks, and lovers once used the dandelion clock as a divination tool to find out where their partner's devotion lay.

Milk thistle

The prickly yet beautiful milk thistle (*Silybum marianum*) is a flowering plant from the Asteraceae, or daisy family. It grows prolifically in Mediterranean countries, North Africa and the Middle East, and if left untended can become impenetrable. The name derives from the leaves, which contain a milky sap and are recognizable by mottled splashes of white. Legend has it that milk fell from the Virgin Mary's breast as she fed baby Jesus onto the milk thistle plant, hence its folk names of Mary's Thistle, Our Lady's Thistle and Holy Thistle.

Those suffering from the previous night's excess will certainly feel that there's something holy about this thistle. It is probably most well-known for its incredible liver healing properties and has been used as a liver tonic for over 2000 years. Milk thistle seeds contain the chemical compound silymarin, which has been shown to have dramatic healing effects on liver stresses ranging from cirrhosis of the liver and hepatitis to gallbladder disorders and patients undergoing chemotherapy. It is the liver that has to deal with the onslaught of coffee, alcohol, drugs, fatty and junk foods, red meat, pesticides and environmental pollutants that our bodies are often subjected to. This is where milk thistle comes into her own – a regular dose dramatically improves liver function.

Primitive negative emotions, such as anger, are stored in the liver. Anger can be useful if it is used productively but it is often difficult to express anger in a healthy way. Sometimes we turn to addictions to block out real emotions. Milk thistle combined with meditation can help us to acknowledge and release anger.

It is thought that milk thistle found its way to Britain when the Roman armies arrived, taking the seeds, leaves, stalks and roots with them to provide food and medicine. The Roman physician and naturalist Pliny the Elder wrote that the juice of the plant, mixed with honey, is excellent for 'carrying off bile' – one of the earliest references to its liver-healing properties.

As its name suggests, milk thistle has been reported to be an effective aid to breast-feeding women, promoting milk flow. Whilst there isn't clear evidence, a history of its use for such a reason is usually a pretty good indicator of its effectiveness. One of the huge benefits of this plant is that it is so safe and can be used by pregnant and breastfeeding women and children. Its detoxifying properties help with skin conditions such as acne, eczema and psoriasis.

It is the black, shiny seeds that are used in most milk thistle preparations that can be purchased from health food shops. They were traditionally roasted and can be used as a coffee substitute. Although it is not so popular now, milk thistle used to be highly regarded as a food and was commonly grown in gardens for that purpose, the flower heads boiled and eaten like artichokes. The shoots are still popular in some countries today and are very palatable and nutritious, generally being cooked and eaten like cabbage. The leaves have a taste similar to spinach and can be used both as a cooked vegetable and as a delicious salad green.

Urinary system

The health of our kidneys is crucial to our wellbeing. They carry out the vital functions of preserving, cleaning and circulating fluids in our bodies. Keeping our fluid levels balanced by drinking enough water and limiting the intake of dehydrating foods and drinks such as coffee and alcohol is essential. A lack of fluid in the body can lead to problems such as dry mouth, headaches, dry and itchy eyes, dry and clicky joints (due to a lack of synovial fluids), dry skin and urinary tract problems.

Drinking the requisite two litres of fresh water a day is vital. As is reducing intake of sugary, fatty foods and trying to reintroduce more healthy, simple fare. Your body won't appreciate going cold turkey on all your usual treats but you can simply add lots of greenery and wholegrains to your diet to begin with. Gradually the body will detox and you will find yourself reaching for more nourishing healthy foods. Pack in more dark green vegetables, nuts, fruit, lean meat and fish to keep your Vitamin B, iron, potassium, magnesium, copper and zinc levels up; and broccoli, cabbage, oranges and berries for Vitamin C.

Kidney imbalance leads to more than just feeling dehydrated. In Chinese medicine, the kidneys and bladder belong to the water element and the emotion related to this area is fear and anxiety. When the water element is balanced in our body and our kidneys are healthy, we have a healthy fear response; when it is out of balance we either have no fear or we live in constant state of anxiety.

The main function of our kidneys is to remove toxins. The ancient practice of reflexology, which has been used for thousands of years to keep the body in balance, can help stimulate the kidneys and keep them in good working condition. Find the kidney points in the centre of the feet. You can use your thumb to apply light pressure on this spot, using a small, circular movement to help boost your kidney function.

There are natural remedies that can be used to improve kidney function – celery seed and fennel are two key plants to use for the urinary system. You'll also be able to read about the incredible healing powers of urine on page 57. If you can get past the squeamishness you'll discover a powerful healer available to you whenever you need it.

Kidney stones

This is a crystallization of the urine, often accompanied by pain and the passing of blood in the urine. Flush the kidneys with lemon juice taken in warm water three times a day. Use essential oil of lemon, fennel and geranium in the bath or a few drops in a carrier oil, such as sweet almond oil, can be massaged into the lower back and bladder area. Make a tonic from celery seeds to benefit the kidneys.

Celery seed tonic

▶ 2 tbsp celery seed
▶ 600 ml (1 pint) brandy

1. Crush the celery seed in a pestle and mortar.
2. Place in a glass jar and cover with the brandy.
3. Leave for two weeks to infuse. Strain and store in a dark bottle.
4. Take 1 tbsp daily mixed with 2 tbsp water to boost kidney function.

Urinary complaints

Drink the water used to cook asparagus to treat general disorders of the urinary system.

Cystitis

An inflammation of the bladder, which causes burning pain when passing urine. The need to pee is frequent although often little, if any, urine is passed. Avoid scented bath products and drink plenty of water to flush the urinary system. Bio live yoghurt can be applied to the vaginal area to encourage good bacteria. Oats are soothing to the system – see page 30 for a calming oat water tonic that can be taken regularly to help flush out the system and soothe inflammation caused by cystitis. Cantharis is the homeopathic remedy for treating cystitis. Cranberry juice or tea can be drunk to help flush out the system.

Stress incontinence

Uncontrollable passing of urine when there is pressure on the abdomen through laughing, sneezing or after childbirth. Drink plenty of water to keep the bladder muscles working. Horsetail is a strengthening herb for the bladder. You can make this herb into a drink to aid bladder control.

Bladder strengthening tea

▶ 1 tsp horsetail, chopped into small pieces
▶ 2 cups water

1. Place the horsetail in a saucepan.
2. Cover with 2 cups of water and heat gently for 30 minutes.
3. Strain and drink a cup, morning and night.

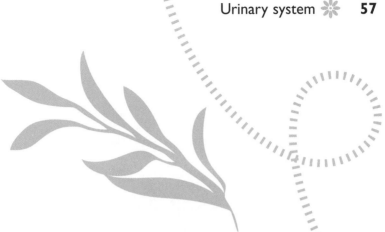

Urine therapy

Your own urine has healing powers. Many people feel uneasy about using what they consider to be a waste product from the body as a therapeutic treatment and I must admit it took me several years to get over the 'Urghh, why would anyone want to do that?' reaction that I had initially. Now that I have tried it on myself for several years and used it for my family too, I understand the healing properties of this gift from our bodies. If you look at the ingredients on many skincare products you'll often find urea listed. This is urine, often sourced from cattle, used for its skin enhancing properties. Applying fresh urine to any cut, wound, burn, insect bite or sting will help the body to heal. I have found it an incredible treatment for many skin problems and effective in treating aches and pains, too.

You can create a urine pack to treat areas of pain or discomfort in the body. When you have a headache for example it is a good idea to place a urine pack on the liver region of the body (just under the ribs). Take a cloth and soak it in your own urine. Place the cloth over the area that you want to treat. Wrap a towel over the top around the body, followed by an old sheet. Place a shower curtain or plastic sheet on the bed and lie down with a hot water bottle on top of the wrapping that covers the urine pack. Rest for 30 minutes. You can use this as often as is required to relieve the pain. Urine is a quick working therapy and many who have tried it see it as a miracle that we have such a strong and effective medicine available to us on tap and for free. Try it!

Nettle

Stinging nettles (*urtica urens*) may not be an obvious choice for a useful and healing garden plant, but they offer many benefits to the gardener. They attract wildlife, can be woven into a strong hardwearing cloth and also have many healing properties.

This plant can be found all over the temperate regions of the world and has much lore and legend attached to it. In Scandinavian mythology the nettle was sacred to Thor, God of Thunder. It was believed that if a plant was thrown onto a fire during a thunderstorm the house would be protected from lightening. Nettles were also thought to bring courage to the bearer and to drive away fearful thoughts in times of danger, so people often carried a small pouch of them if they were heading off on a long journey.

Romans reputedly planted nettles along the roadsides in Britain to warm themselves up. They thought that it would be so cold in Britain's chilly climes that they would need to thrash themselves with nettles to warm the blood. Native American Indians believed that the leaves held special powers and they were used in the treatment of aches and pains, while European herbalists were using the leaves in similar ways on the other side of the Atlantic to relieve gout and arthritis.

An irritant found in the tiny hairs found on the leaf and stem – histamine – causes the sting. Each hair is hollow with the venom stored at its base. When the hair is brushed against, it breaks off exposing a sharp point which penetrates the skin and delivers the sting.

How wonderfully clever nature is to invent such a complex weapon against predators and then to counteract this with an offering of dock leaves, which can usually be found growing nearby. The leaves of dock, when rubbed on the affected area, release a chemical that neutralizes the sting and soothes the skin.

Nettles have long been used as food and even Pepys wrote of eating '…some nettle porridge, which was very good.' This plant is an excellent source of calcium, iron, magnesium and a range of vitamins. Young nettles can be gathered (whilst wearing gloves) and steeped in a pot of boiling water to create an excellent spring tonic, which helps to clear out the toxins accumulated during the winter months. When dried or cooked, the nettle loses its sting. Nettle tea has many beneficial uses, such as treatment of rheumatism and urinary disorders and it is also a rich source of iron and calcium for pregnant women. It can be used to good effect after birth too as it stimulates milk flow in lactating mothers. Nettle tea has also been shown to be beneficial in treating skin rashes.

To get a nettle patch started in your garden, look for a sunny sheltered spot and ensure that the soil is well nourished. Find a friend who can donate some plants for your plot – an allotment owner or keen gardener should be only too happy to give you some. Nettles are wild so should not be taken from the countryside. Plant the nettles about 30 cm (11¾ in) apart and keep them well watered. It is a good idea to fix a path or boundary around your patch as nettles can quickly take over. Then sit back and watch your garden thrive and your health blossom as you use this powerful cleansing, balancing plant.

Respiratory system

Respiratory problems of all kinds can respond really well to alternative therapies. The two most common problems affecting the nose are the common cold and hayfever. Colds can be treating very effectively with herbs – there are a number of decongestant plants that can be used. Sometimes on an unconscious level when we are disappointed or disillusioned we develop colds and sinus problems. The nose being blocked can represent a holding on to tears due to holding on to grief or disappointment.

The remedies in this section can help balance the emotions and unblock the nose. You'll find out how to make a peppermint steam bath to clear the nasal passages and find ways of treating build-up of catarrh and sinusitis. For hayfever, the traditional remedy is a teaspoon of local honey taken every morning upon waking, before the season begins. Elderflower is also a very effective remedy and you'll find a recipe that you can use to make your own tea, which can be taken internally to lessen the severity of your symptoms.

Common cold

An infection of the upper respiratory tract, which is very common, especially during the winter months. Excess mucus is produced and the usual symptoms are a runny nose, sore throat and coughing. Colds can also produce a fever, which the body's natural way of fighting an infection. Work with the body rather than against it when a fever sets in. The most important thing to remember is the body's need for rest when an infection such as a cold takes over. If you do not allow yourself to deal with the infection naturally, if you suppress it with painkillers or decongestant drugs, then you will just be burying the problem and it will crop up again at a later date as you won't have given your body a chance to remove unwanted toxins from the system. The quickest method for treating a cold is to make a honey and lemon tea.

Add the juice of half a lemon and a teaspoon of honey to a cup of boiling water. Allow to cool slightly and drink. Take as often as needed. You can also make a honey and onion syrup to treat coughs and colds.

Honey and onion syrup

1. Slice an onion finely and lay in a shallow bowl.
2. Cover with honey and leave overnight.
3. In the morning, pour off the liquid and use as needed.
4. 1 tbsp can be taken three times a day to treat a common cold.

Sinusitis

Inflammation of the sinuses – the air filled cavities around the nose – that causes a blocked uncomfortable feeling. A peppermint steam bath can be beneficial to help release the blockage. You can also try this with essential oil of lavender, eucalyptus and tea tree. Lavender acts as an anti-inflammatory and will ease any pain. Elderflower is the plant traditionally used to treat sinusitis. You can make a nose wash using the flowers, which grace the hedgerows in late spring.

Elderflower nasal wash

1. Take two sprigs of flowers and place in a cup.
2. Cover with boiling water and allow to cool slightly.
3. Add a pinch of salt.
4. Take the cup to the nose and sniff through each nostril in turn.
5. This can be practiced morning and evening to relieve symptoms.

Peppermint steam bath

1. Take a handful of fresh peppermint leaves.
2. Cover with boiling water.
3. Place a towel over your head.
4. Lean over the bowl and inhale the steam from the peppermint.

Catarrh

An over production of thick phlegm by the mucous membranes, this is often the result of a heavy cold. Many aromatherapy oils are decongestants. Make a blend using 1 cup carrier oil such as organic sweet almond oil, add 2 drops of camomile, pine or clary sage. Rub this into the temples. You can also use these oils in a steam bath. Take a large bowl, fill with boiling water, add a few drops of your chosen oil, lean over and inhale the steam. Make a mustard footbath to warm the body and help to decongest the nasal passages.

Mustard foot bath

1. Fill a washing up bowl with hot water.
2. Add 1 teaspoon of mustard powder and stir to disperse.
3. Place feet in the bowl and stay for 15 minutes or until water starts to cool.

Flu

Viral disease of the upper respiratory tract resulting in fever, aching limbs, runny nose, sore throat and sometimes nausea and loss of appetite. It is important to allow the body to rest completely and to keep fluid levels up. Barley water can be used to treat respiratory disorders and is also useful in easing a dry tickly cough.

Barley water

1. Add 2 tbsp barley to 600 ml (1 pint) water.
2. Boil for 10 minutes.
3. Strain through a muslin cloth and add the barley to a fresh pint of water.
4. Boil this batch for 10 minutes.
5. Strain and drink warm or cold, as often as required. Add lemon and honey to taste, if desired.

Hayfever

An allergic reaction to airborne irritants such as pollen. Swelling of the nasal passages accompanies red itchy eyes. Symptoms include sneezing and a runny nose. Lots of sufferers use local honey to treat hayfever. Take a teaspoon every day to ease symptoms. Eyebright tea can be used to soothe itchy eyes. Make an elderflower tea that can be taken internally to strengthen the immune system and help to prevent hayfever. The flowers can also be enjoyed fresh to relieve the symptoms.

Elderflower tea

1. Take a handful of elderflower flowers and place in a cup.
2. Cover with boiling water.
3. Place a plate over the cup and leave to infuse for 10 minutes.
4. Drink whilst still warm, up to three cups a day.

Nosebleeds

Sometimes caused by infection of the mucous membrane. Massage a drop of lavender into the nostril to help the area to heal and to stop the flow of blood. Lean forward and lightly pinch the bridge of the nose to ease the flow. Take rescue remedy in cases of emotional distress.

Sore throat

Inflammation of the throat caused by infection. Pain with difficulty in swallowing, sometimes accompanied by a fever, earache and hoarseness. Lymph nodes in the neck become enlarged and tender. Gargle with honey water to soothe the throat. Add 1 tablespoon of honey to a cup of warm water, stir to dissolve and then gargle with the liquid. Drink a hot honey and lemon tea before bed to ease symptoms and encourage a restful night's sleep.

Coughs

This is an action taken by the body to remove foreign bodies and mucus from the airways. Make a garlic tincture to treat coughs. This will help the body fight infection.

Honey and lemon tea

1. Place the juice of ½ lemon and 1 tbsp of honey in a cup.
2. Top with boiling water.
3. Allow to cool and then drink.

Apple cider vinegar compress

Apply an apple cider vinegar compress to the throat area to ease a sore throat.

1. Pour ½ cup of cider vinegar into a large bowl.
2. Top up with boiling water.
3. Leave to infuse for 10 minutes.
4. Soak a cloth in the liquid, wring out and apply to the throat area.
5. Lie down and relax for 15 minutes with the compress on the throat.

Garlic tincture

1. Place 5 peeled garlic cloves in a glass jar.
2. Cover with organic vodka or brandy and seal.
3. Leave to infuse for 2 weeks.
4. Strain and take a tsp as required to ease a cough. Can be taken up to three times a day.

Pneumonia

An infection of the lung caused by bacteria or virus entering the upper respiratory tract. This results in inflammation of the lung tissue. Rapid shallow breathing, chest pain, sore throat and fever accompany. Raw garlic in the diet will help aid the body in fighting the infection. To help ease the breathing, make a steam bath using eucalyptus and tea tree essential oils. Add a few drops of each to a bowl of boiling water. Take a towel, place over your head and inhale the steam.

Asthma

Inflammation of the lining of the airways, which results in restriction of airflow and breathing difficulty. Make a steam inhalation of lavender, camomile or eucalyptus to help open the airways. Take a few drops of rescue remedy on the tongue at the start of an attack to help lessen the effects.

Lung infection/bronchitis

Inflammation of the lining of the air tubes of the lungs. Can cause chest pain, fever, wheezing and shortness of breath and a hacking cough. Liquorice root is beneficial in the treatment of bronchitis. Mix 1 teaspoon powdered root with 1 tablespoon of honey and take every morning for up to two weeks. Lung disorders can be treated with garlic syrup.

Garlic syrup

1. Peel and crush 8 cloves of garlic.
2. Place in a glass jar and cover with 10 tbsp honey.
3. Allow to stand for several days.
4. Use as needed (1 tsp children, 4 tsp for adults, twice daily).

Lavender

Lavender is an evergreen woody shrub, which grows up to 1 metre (1 yard) tall, with pale green, narrow leaves and flowers of a beautiful violet/blue colour. It has an immediately recognisable scent when you gently press the flower spike between you finger and thumb. Endowed with both antiseptic and sedative properties, lavender's supreme versatility has led some to call it nature's medicine chest. Almost everyone is familiar with the smell of the lavender plant, and it has over 2,500 years of recorded use as a strewing herb, a mood tonic, a fragrance, an insect repellent, a medicine and a food flavouring. The 28 different species of lavender are grown for their flowers and for their essential oil.

In ancient times lavender was used for mummification and perfume by the Egyptians, Phoenicians and peoples of Arabia. The Greeks and the Romans bathed in lavender scented water and it was from the Latin word *lavo* meaning 'to wash' that the herb took its name. Lavender has long been used to clean and heal wounds – the Romans used it for this purpose and in more recent history, nurses used it for the wounded soldiers during the Second World War.

Lavender has many royal connections. Queen Elizabeth I valued lavender as a conserve and a perfume. Her love of lavender was such that she is supposed to have commanded her gardeners to ensure that fresh lavender flowers should be available all year round. She also used lavender infused in hot water to make a tea to help ease her migraines. Queen Victoria also had a passion for this plant and is responsible for making lavender popular as a perfume. She used it in every one of her rooms, for washing floors and furniture, freshening the air, and for scattering amongst the linens.

The 17th century medical herbalist Nicholas Culpeper recommended this plant for a variety of ailments, including pains of the head, cramps and fainting. Lavender is one of the main essential oils and is something of a mini medicine chest. It is an invaluable oil to have around the house for any number of little, and large, emergencies. The oil can be dabbed neat onto the skin immediately after burning to speed up the skin's healing processes, and for this reason alone it is an essential part of any home first-aid kit. The essential oil of lavender can also be used to ease stress and anxiety and is best used in a burner or vaporizer to promote a calm and peaceful environment.

For colds, flu and catarrh, try adding two drops of lavender oil to a bowl of boiled water and putting your head over the steam for about five minutes to inhale the healing properties. One of the most soothing uses for lavender is in a hot compress for period and labour pains, arthritis and headaches. Add 5–6 drops of lavender oil to a bowl of warm water, swish a soft flannel in the liquid, squeeze out any excess fluid and then hold over the affected area until the flannel has cooled. Repeat as needed. A cold compress is another way to reap the benefits of lavender and more useful for sprains, burns and scalds, insect bites, stings and sunburn. Repeat the above steps but use cold water. A cool flannel infused with lavender is a great comfort when your skin is taut and painful after over-exposure to the sun.

Lavender is also one of the few oils that can be used neat (without dilution in a base oil) on the skin. It can be dabbed directly onto spots, boils, cuts, grazes, burns, insect bites, acne, and other skin conditions. A few drops on a handkerchief or tissue can be used to calm symptoms of sudden stress, panic, hysteria, shock and butterflies in the stomach.

You can grow your own lavender plants for use in food and for pot pourri and linen. The tender varieties such as French and Spanish lavender can be grown outside in pots in summer, then brought inside to a bright windowsill for the winter. The soil in the pot should contain some sand to aid drainage. While these varieties are not as fragrant as the hardy lavenders, they will reward you with blooms almost all year-round. Harvest lavender for drying when the first bud on the flower stalk is starting to open. To dry, bind stems with a rubber band or string and hang in a warm, dry, dark spot. When dry, pack away in boxes or plastic bags for medicinal or culinary use.

The skin

Our skin is the organ most in touch with the outside world. It protects us from our environment, releases toxins and keeps our body temperature in balance by opening and closing pores and releasing sweat to cool the body.

Spots, sweating, hair loss and rashes are usually symptoms of other, deeper seated problems – for example acne is often caused by a hormone imbalance. Sweating disorders include a lack of sweating or excess sweating. In Traditional Chinese medicine, excess heat in the body can lead to dryness, itching, redness and flaking of skin cells. Cooling herbs and foods such as cucumber and mint can be taken regularly to balance the body temperature.

The skin is the largest organ of the body. The bowels excrete waste, the kidneys excrete fluids, lungs excrete gases, and skin excretes anything else. Therefore skin symptoms present when there is an imbalance in the body. Eczema, psoriasis and other skin conditions often result when the other elimination channels are blocked.

Skin rashes can be an allergic reaction to an outside agent (such as perfumed soap, deodorants, washing powders, textiles, metals in clothing); they can result from foods or medications or drugs, or be a reaction to something the body does not tolerate.

In this chapter you can find out how to make your own deodorant to treat excess perspiration, try a soothing oatmeal bath to ease the symptoms of eczema and use plantain to heal insect bites and stings.

Eczema

This is a skin inflammation that is visible
through red cracked patches of skin,
common on hands, feet and behind the
ears. The symptoms are burning, itching
skin with a desire to scratch. Sometimes
the skin blisters and these can open and
weep. See pages 120–121 for advice on
how to treat children's eczema. The
essential oil of camomile can be very
soothing to irritated skin. Add a few drops

Oatmeal bath

1. Take a handful of oats and place in
the centre of a square of muslin
cloth.
2. Gather the oats in the muslin cloth
3. Secure with a piece of string or a
rubber band and place in a warm
bath.

to 100 ml (3½ fl oz) organic olive oil to make a massage treatment.
Massage into the affected areas. Oats can be used to make a soothing bath
treatment, which calms red, itchy skin and is especially beneficial before
bed to help aid a restful night's sleep.

Psoriasis

A skin disorder that tends to run in families, psoriasis presents as patches
of red skin with a scaly silvery surface. Often affects the armpits and
insides of the knees and elbows. There are ways to treat the irritated skin
with natural remedies but as with all skin disorders,
psoriasis is symptomatic of an imbalance in the body so it
is worth looking at what this might be. Does the
condition flare up at times of stress or when you eat
certain foods, for example? If you can identify the
trigger it will help you to address the problem
holistically. Use the cleansing powers of
garlic by including more of it in your diet.
It is particularly beneficial eaten raw, so
grate into salads or soups just before
serving. Nettle tea helps to cleanse the
system and is especially useful in the spring
and early summer.

Prickly heat

A heat rash that occurs in particularly hot and humid weather. Chickweed ointment can be massaged into the affected area and helps to calm irritated skin. A massage with organic sweet almond oil combined with a few drops of lavender can be a beneficial treatment.

Perspiration

Excessive sweating is usually caused by the body's need to regulate temperature. Commercial anti-perspirants work by blocking the sweat ducts under your armpits. Sweat is your body's way of removing toxins from the body so daily blocking of this simple and effective strategy is not ideal and can cause longer term health problems. It is bacteria mixing with your sweat, rather than the sweat itself, that causes body odour and these deodorants will work to mask this smell.

Deodorant

Baking soda works wonders as it neutralizes the odour of sweat. Just sprinkle a light covering onto a damp flannel and pat on. There is no need to rinse.

Deodorant powder

▶ 8 tbsp baking soda
▶ 8 tbsp cornstarch
▶ A few drops of lavender or lemon essential oils

1. Place the baking soda, cornstarch and essential oils in a glass jar.
2. Shake to blend.
3. Sprinkle a light covering of the powder on to a flannel. and pat on. Do not rinse.

Liquid deodorant

▶ 4 tbsp each of witch hazel extract, aloe vera gel and mineral water
▶ 1 tsp vegetable glycerin
▶ A few drops of lavender or tea tree essential oils

1. Put all of the ingredients in a spray bottle and shake to blend.
2. Spray on as needed.

Acne

Our skin has sebaceous glands that secret an oily substance. Sometimes these glands get over active and secrete excessive oil and that causes acne. Prepare a facial steam bath to draw out infection. Comfrey ointment can be used to reduce acne scarring.

Facial steam bath

▶ A handful each of the flowers of chickweed, elderflower and calendula

1. Fill a bowl with hot water and add the flowers.
2. Place a towel over your head and inhale the steam for 10 minutes.
3. Repeat daily to improve the health of your skin.

Comfrey ointment

▶ 500 g (1¼ lb) beeswax
▶ 60 g (2¼ oz) dried or 150 g (5 oz) fresh comfrey leaves, finely chopped

1. Melt the beeswax in a glass bowl over a pan of boiling water.
2. Add the comfrey leaves and simmer, stirring continuously, for about 1 hour.
3. Pour the mixture into a muslin bag.
4. Wearing rubber gloves, squeeze the mixture through the bag into a jug.
5. Pour the ointment into a jar before it sets. Place the lid on the jar, without securing it.
6. When cool, tighten the lid. Store in a refrigerator for up to 3 months.

Athlete's foot

A fungal infection that grows in the warm, moist skin between the toes. Apply a garlic poultice directly to the affected area. Crush two cloves of garlic, place on the foot and secure with a plaster. Leave on for as long as possible, up to one hour. Make a footbath using essential oils with anti-fungal properties.

Anti-fungal footbath

▶ A few drops each of lavender, tea tree and patchouli essential oils

1. Fill a large bowl with hot water and add the essential oils.
2. Place your feet in the bowl and relax for 15 minutes.

Chilblains

Circular red swelling that usually appearing on the toes, but can affect the hands too, during cold weather. Caused by poor circulation, or the narrowing of the arteries in cold conditions, restricting the flow of blood. Encourage the circulatory system by drinking warming teas such as ginger and rosemary. Make a poultice out of crushed horseradish root and apply to the affected area to encourage healing.

Cuts and sores

When the surface of the skin is damaged it can result in an infection, and the surrounding area becomes red and sore. Make a poultice of cabbage leaves by crushing in a pestle and mortar to release the beneficial juices. Apply to the affected area to draw out the infection and aid healing. Yarrow is also very beneficial in the treatment of cuts and sores. Make your own yarrow tincture, which can be diluted 1 part to 10 parts water. Soak a cloth in the liquid and bathe the wound with it.

Yarrow tincture

1. Pick the flowing tops of the yarrow plant, white ones only, when in bloom.
2. Fill, but don't stuff, a jar, with the coarsely chopped herb.
3. Fill jar to the top with alcohol such as organic vodka.
4. Cap tightly. The yarrow tincture will be ready to use in 6 weeks.

Cold sores

Fluid-filled blisters caused by a viral infection (herpes simplex). Usually appear around the mouth, on the lips or under the nose. They are very contagious and can be painful. Often a symptom of high levels of stress or feeling run down. As soon as it appears, apply St. John's Wort tincture to the cold sore. Place a few drops of lemon juice on the core sore every day until it goes. Lemons have antiseptic and anti-fungal properties.

St. John's Wort tincture

▶ A handful of flowering tops from the St. John's Wort plant
▶ 200 ml (7 fl oz) alcohol, such as organic vodka
▶ 100 ml (3½ fl oz) water

1. Place the flowering tops in a large glass jar.
2. Cover with the alcohol and water.
3. Replace the lid and leave for 2 weeks, shaking occasionally.
4. Strain through a sieve with a muslin cloth inside.
5. Pour the liquid into a clean dark glass bottle and store for up to 1 year.

Sunstroke

Sunstroke occurs when the body becomes overheated through over-exposure to the sun and the brain cannot control the cooling process. Sunstroke is different from and more dangerous than heat stroke. Both conditions cause confusion, light-headedness and fatigue, and shade and cool water on the skin helps. Peppermint has a cooling, soothing effect when taken internally. Drink a cooling tea to help your body get back to its regular temperature.

Cooling tea

1. Take a handful of peppermint leaves, place in a cup and cover with boiling water.
2. Allow to cool.
3. Add the juice of half a lemon and place in the refrigerator.
4. When ready to drink, add ice.

Rashes

A rash is a red eruption of the skin that changes the way the skin looks and feels. Rashes can be localized to one area or may be widespread. Plantain is a wonder plant when it comes to skin problems. Apply this soothing lotion to areas of irritable skin and to treat rashes.

Healing skin lotion

1. Take two handfuls of plantain leaves and crush in a pestle with a mortar.
2. Place in a glass jar and add glycerine (available from chemists) to cover the leaves.
3. Leave for two weeks, stirring occasionally.
4. Strain and store in a dark glass bottle.
5. Use as needed to treat irritable skin conditions.

Warts

A hard raised growth on the skin is referred to as a wart. Warts come in various sizes and shapes and they can affect any age group. They usually grow to certain size and then stop. They commonly appear on the neck, fingers, face, scalp and pretty much any other part of the skin. They sometimes disappear on their own but rubbing freshly squeezed lemon juice into the skin every day can aid the healing process. Eat plenty of garlic and apply a slice of cut garlic to the wart in the evening, secured with a plaster or piece of cloth wrapped and tied around to keep it secure. Use the sap from a dandelion plant to remove warts. Squeeze the milky sap from the stem of a large leaf. Apply once a day until the wart heals.

Boils

An infected hair follicle with a swollen pus-filled area. A painful red lump later becomes a yellow-headed spot. Most commonly occurring under the arms, back of the neck and in the groin. Make a boil treatment using thyme leaves, soak a cloth in it and apply to the boil.

Boil treatment

1. Gather a handful of thyme leaves and place in a cup.
2. Cover with boiling water and allow to steep for 10 minutes.
3. Soak a cloth in the liquid and apply to the affected area.

Hair loss

We shed 150 hairs a day but this number can be increased by stress. Rosemary is a traditional hair tonic. Massage a few drops of rosemary essential oil into the scalp. It is said that the increased flow of blood to the head in positions such as shoulder stand in yoga can have a beneficial effect on hair growth. You can even reap the benefits during a supported leg raise. Find a wall with no obstructions and lie on your back with your legs raised at right angles up the wall. Drink a regular cup of sage tea to stimulate hair growth.

Sage tea

1. Take a handful of sage leaves and place in a cup.
2. Cover with boiling water, place a plate over the top and leave to infuse for ten minutes.
3. Drink a cup every morning – up to three cups a day.

Dandruff

When the scalp sheds dead skin cells in large clumps, the flakes can get trapped in the hair and accumulate with oil and dirt to cause dandruff. Scaling maybe accompanied by mild itching, causing redness and flaking. Dandruff can also occur in the eyebrows. Rosemary is the traditional treatment for itchy, irritable scalps and dandruff.

Rosemary vinegar

▶ 25 g (1 oz) chopped fresh rosemary
▶ 1.2 lt (2 pt) cider vinegar

1. Place the rosemary in a large glass jar and cover with the cider vinegar.
2. Leave for 2 weeks, shaking occasionally.
3. Strain and bottle the liquid.
4. Massage 2 tbsp into the hair, half an hour before washing.

Sunburn

Spending too long in the sun can cause the skin to burn. It feels hot, tingly and uncomfortable and becomes red and hot to the touch. Calendula oil is soothing to the system and helps the skin to heal effectively and prevent scarring. Take a cool bath, gently massage the oil into the affected areas and then rest.

Calendula oil

▶ A handful of dried calendula flowers
▶ Enough sweet almond oil or apricot kernel oil to fill your jar

1. Place the dried flowers in a glass jar with a lid and cover completely with the oil.
2. Seal tightly and leave to infuse for 3 to 8 weeks, shaking daily.
3. When the oil has turned golden, strain through a piece of muslin and bottle it in a dark glass bottle. Store in the refrigerator and use to treat skin conditions such as wounds, spots and sunburn.

Insect bites

These are very common from late spring through to autumn. Use a burner to diffuse essential oil of citronella on summer evenings or use citronella candles. Some people find that eating plenty of garlic keeps the mosquitoes away while others apply lemon juice to their skin to act as a preventative barrier.

Insect repellent

Rub lemon juice, a natural insect-icide, into the skin to discourage mosquitoes and other small biting insects.

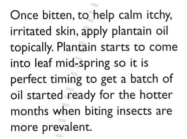

Once bitten, to help calm itchy, irritated skin, apply plantain oil topically. Plantain starts to come into leaf mid-spring so it is perfect timing to get a batch of oil started ready for the hotter months when biting insects are more prevalent.

Plantain oil

Choose a dry, sunny day and harvest the plantain in the afternoon (once the dew has dried).

1. Tightly pack a clean, dry jar full of plantain leaves and fill with olive oil.
2. Place the jar out of direct sunlight and store at room temperature for 3 weeks, topping the oil up so that it completely covers the leaves every day for the first week.
3. Strain the oil and apply to itchy, irritated skin.

Calendula

Also known as the Pot Marigold, *Calendula officinalis* is an easy-to-grow plant, which has numerous uses and healing properties. The vibrant orange and yellow flowers are said to lift the spirits and encourage cheerfulness. However, this colourful flowering plant is perhaps best known for its skin healing properties. It can be used to treat wounds, burns, insect bites, eczema, skin ulcers and rashes. Indeed many herbalists use calendula in their preparations, and anthroscopic medicinal producer Weleda have a special range of soothing calendula products. An infusion of the petals can be used for flu and fevers as it helps to induce perspiration. For ear infections, a drop of oil on a cotton ball can be effective. The soothing properties of calendula can also be useful to treat sore nipples and nappy rash.

The plant is grown easily from seed in spring and while calendula prefers rich well-drained soil, it is very tolerant of poor soils. Choose a sunny spot and you can enjoy the pleasure of growing your own medicine. As the plant flowers, pinch the heads and leave these to dry in a cool place out of direct sunlight and free from moisture. Regular harvesting of the flowers increases production. Store the dried flower heads in jars and use as needed. Be sure to leave some flower heads at the end of the flowering season so that you can collect the seeds and start afresh next year.

It is thought that the calendula plant originated in the Mediterranean and North Africa, and it was certainly valued highly by the Ancient Egyptians and Romans when it was known as the 'Herb of the Sun'. In Christianity, the flower was associated with the Virgin Mary, from which the common name Marigold (Mary Gold) is derived. In addition to healing humans, Calendula has also been used to treat animals for centuries. Three handfuls of flowers mixed with their food twice daily is said to aid heart problems, vomiting and skin conditions. A lotion can be made to treat bee and wasp stings by boiling chopped leaves and flowers in milk.

The petals of calendula flowers have long been used to flavour foods. When fresh they have a very mild flavour but once cooked impart a savoury taste, which complements soups, stews and baked foods like bread and scones. In the summer, the flower heads make a beautiful addition to salads. A preserve can be made by placing whole leaves and petals in a wide-mouthed jar. Cover with sugar and leave until a syrup forms. Fresh calendula flowers heighten the energy in a room and have been used to attract and see the fairies! Placed under a pillow before bed, the flowers apparently encourage clairvoyancy and petals scattered under the bed protect you in your sleep and make your dreams come true. A truly magical bright flower that deserves a sunny spot in your garden.

Heart and blood health

Heart attack rates are increasing, with significantly higher rates for men. The typical causes are smoking, high cholesterol, high blood pressure and obesity, all of which are as prevalent in women as they are in men. So why the gender divide?

One theory is that men need to change the way that they deal with emotions in order to start healing their hearts. The heart is incredibly sensitive to stress, and many systems of medicine recommend that we regularly take notice of the feelings and functions of the heart and care for this strong but sensitive muscle.

This school of thought believes that the emotional reserve of many men begins in childhood when they receive less physical affection and hugging than their female siblings. The giving and receiving of affection in the form of touch and embrace conveys positive emotions and nourishes the heart. Perhaps if men were encouraged to express their emotions more readily heart disease would be less prevalent. Tears should be allowed to flow freely to express feelings of happiness and experiences of frustration, grief and pain. If we can begin to see crying as a healthy response to life, it will help us to rid the body's build-up of stress. Suppressing tears is likely to increase the body's susceptibility to illness and blocking emotions can contribute to hypertension or high blood pressure.

Nourishing the heart

Get in balance Express yourself – both the positive and the negative feelings and emotions.

Laugh and play Balance productivity with playfulness. Scientific studies have shown that laughter boosts the immune system by replacing hormones that act as immune suppressants.

Keep fit Exercise develops the muscles and provides the rhythmic contraction and relaxation of the skeletal muscles that help circulate blood.

Eat simply Eat wholegrains, vegetables and organic proteins. Avoid excess salt, sugar, additives and processed food.

Use herbs Plants that are especially good for the heart muscle are hawthorn, motherwort, yarrow, garlic, ginger and cayenne.

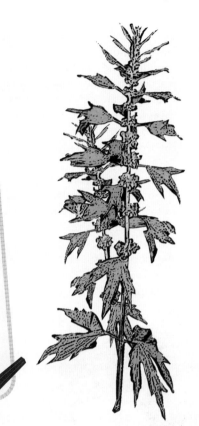

Of course, a strong heart is necessary to keep limbs and organs in shape, and, equally, to help us cope with life's ups and downs. The way we use or abuse it has serious long-term effects on our health. Every time we make a decision to walk in the park, go for a swim or a run, or just choose the life option that makes us truly happy, we are doing our hearts good. Left neglected for too long, we run the risk not only physically of developing life threatening diseases – particularly of arteries, the blood vessels that supply all the body's cells with nutrients and oxygen – but also depression and anxiety. Diet and coping mechanisms are the first line of defence.

Starting with diet, reduce your intake of saturated fat and eat plenty of fresh fruit and vegetables, which are high in antioxidants, as well as magnesium, calcium and potassium, which are all important heart nutrients. Foods that are rich in magnesium include tofu, beans, seeds, almonds, cashews, buckwheat, garlic, whole grains, green leafy vegetables and potato skins – next time you have a baked potato, make sure you eat the whole thing.

Increase the amounts of essential fats, especially the omega 3 essential fats, found in oily fish such as salmon, mackerel, tuna, herring, linseeds, walnuts, pumpkin seeds, soya, and green leafy vegetables. Garlic can help lower the blood pressure by dilating the blood vessels, and can be added raw to natural low fat yogurt.

Antioxidant nutrients, such as beta-carotene, selenium, Vitamin E and Vitamin C are important in protecting against the development of heart disease. They help prevent something called free radical damage. Fats and cholesterol are particularly susceptible to free radical damage – damage caused by toxins like cigarette smoke. This 'damaged' cholesterol is much more dangerous to the heart and circulation system.

In this section I look at ways to treat heart problems such as hypertension and angina. The most effective herb for heart health is probably the hawthorn. Its berries and leaves can be used to make a range of natural remedies to improve heart health.

High blood pressure

Also known as hypertension, which can cause headaches, shortness of breath and visual disturbances. Raw garlic is used as a tonic to the circulatory system – ensure that you get lots in your diet. Regular massage, especially around the shoulders, middle back and chest area can be very beneficial. Use oils such as lavender and ylang ylang. Hawthorn berries can be used to treat heart problems. Gather in the autumn months when the hedgerows are full of the deep red fruit.

Hawthorn berry brandy

1. Pack several handfuls of leaves and berries into a large glass jar.
2. Cover with brandy and leave in a cool dark place for two weeks.
3. Strain the liquid into dark bottles and take 2 tbsp daily as a heart tonic.

Low blood pressure

Also known as hypotension, this is a rapid drop in blood pressure. Many people experience it when standing up quickly. It is important to stimulate the circulation in order to avoid dizziness and fainting. Regular aerobic exercise is a good idea for everyone, but especially those suffering from hypotension. If you feel faint when you stand up quickly, lower your chin to your chest until the feeling subsides. Warming herbs such as rosemary and ginger are useful and can be made into a tea. Steep a tablespoon of grated ginger in a cup of boiling water and drink to improve circulation. Massage with warming oils, such as black pepper and rosemary will help stimulate and warm the body.

Anaemia

This is usually caused by an iron deficiency either through surgery, trauma or childbirth. Nettle tea is an excellent tonic for those suffering from anaemia.

Nettle tea

1. Put on a pair of gloves and collect a handful of young nettle tops
2. Place in a cup, pour over boiling water.
3. Place a plate over the top and leave to infuse for ten minutes.
4. Strain and drink while still warm.

Angina

Chest pain caused by the narrowing of the arteries. Pain occurs after exertion or a heavy meal. Motherwort is a wild plant that helps to calm the heart. It can be taken as a tea (see page 113). Hawthorn is another good treatment for angina. Make an infusion of the berries and take as a tonic.

Hawthorn infusion

1. Take a handful of berries and leaves and place them in a cup.
2. Pour over boiling water to cover.
3. Leave to infuse for ten minutes.
4. Strain and drink. Enjoy three cups a day as a heart tonic.

Varicose veins

Swollen veins, often occurring in the legs or in the rectum (haemorrhoids). Drink beetroot juice daily as it is strengthening to the system. Massage legs affected by varicose veins with a rosemary blend. Add three drops of rosemary essential oil to a cup of organic sweet almond oil. Massage with long strokes into the affected area. A witch hazel compress can ease aching varicose veins.

Witch hazel compress

▶ 25 g (1 oz) cut witch hazel bark
▶ 500 ml (18 fl oz) water

1. Place the witch hazel bark into a saucepan and pour over the water.
2. Simmer gently for 10 minutes.
3. Allow to cool and then strain.
4. Soak a cloth in the liquid and apply to the affected area. You can leave it on for half an hour, re-soaking the cloth as needed.

Haemorrhoids

The primary cause of haemorrhoids is chronic constipation, straining and the pressure this causes on the surrounding veins. Haemorrhoids are common during pregnancy and in conditions affecting the liver and upper bowel. Pain at passing stools, slight bleeding in the case of internal trouble, and feeling of soreness and irritation after passing a stool are the usual symptoms. Cut a slim piece of potato and insert it into the anus to ease discomfort. Use witch hazel to make a compress and sit on it to reduce inflammation and swelling. Add rosemary essential oil to a warm bath as a soothing treatment before bed. Haemorrhoids can also be treated using the appropriately named pilewort. This plant is also known as lesser celandine (not to be confused with greater celandine) and can be found in wooded areas in the spring.

Pilewort compress

▶ 25 g (1 oz) pilewort root
▶ 500 ml (18 fl oz) water

1. Place the pilewort root into a saucepan and pour over the water.
2. Simmer gently for 10 minutes.
3. Allow to cool and then strain.
4. Soak a cloth in the liquid and apply to the affected area. You can leave it on for half an hour, re-soaking the cloth as needed.

Hawthorn

Hawthorn (*Crataegus*) is synonymous with mid Spring and is steeped in magic and mystery. With its beautiful flowers and sharp thorns, the hawthorn is a paradox of a plant. It has long been revered for its magical properties and has been loved and respected throughout history. It is found throughout Britain, Europe, western Asia and North Africa and grows to between 5 and 15 metres (5½ to 16½ yards) tall. It is popular as a hedge plant and many animals and birds make their homes in its dense thorny twigs. The fruit are sometimes known as 'haws', and this is where the hawthorn gets its name. The thorns are usually 1–3 cm (½–1 in) long, so you know when you've been pricked by one!

Hawthorns have been known to live for 400 years and clumps of twisted old trees can be found in towns, reminders of where old hedgerows were situated. The light, hard wood from the Hawthorn provides the hottest fire known.

Hawthorn is the sixth tree of the Celtic Tree Ogham. It represents love, fertility, the heart, protection, the release of blocked energy and preparation for spiritual growth. For this reason, hawthorn has an affinity with the Celtic festival Beltane – the Hawthorn's Spring blossom was used to decorate and celebrate this fertile time of year. Before the church discredited Spring customs, Hawthorn played a valuable part in May Day celebrations, when the union of the May Queen and the Green Man blessed the fertility of the Earth. However, the folk customs lived on and marriages continued to take place at this special, abundant time of year. Newly married couples would find garlands of mayflowers decorating their beds, representing fertility and lasting love. The maypole was traditionally a living Hawthorn tree, brought into the village and danced around in order to bring life, love and fertility to a community. A sprig of Hawthorn is said to promote happiness in the troubled, depressed or sad.

Legend has it that young women bathed in the dew of Hawthorn as a beauty aid. Hawthorn has long been associated with the fairy realm, and there is much lore and legend surrounding it. A tea made of the leaves and blossoms is said to aid anxiety, appetite loss and poor circulation, and this special plant has strong links with spirituality. Solitary hawthorns often marked old sacred groves or meeting places, wells, springs, underground water and fairy places. Where groups of hawthorn trees grew in threes, they would be treated with great respect. Enchantment was said to be the result of lingering under these trees. It has long been considered bad luck to uproot or disturb a hawthorn tree and cuttings were only made on 1st May, or Beltane. Hawthorn is also recognized as a protective plant and charms were made by twisting the branches into globes, which were hung in houses and in babies' cradles. In Ireland, people would tie ribbons and rags ('clouties') to hawthorn trees situated near sacred wells, as gifts to the fairies and tree spirits. These gifts were said to attract love and healing to the giver and symbolize a wish made. A pink ribbon was used to wish for love, a blue ribbon to wish for protection, a green ribbon to wish for wealth and a purple or indigo ribbon to wish for greater knowledge. Love and respect for this plant did not die out with the arrival of the Christians – Jesus' crown of thorns was said to be a wreath of Hawthorn and the Burning Bush seen by Moses a hawthorn bush.

Hawthorn also has culinary and herbal uses. The berries have been used as a cardiac tonic for centuries and the leaves as a substitute for oriental green tea. A tea made of the leaves and blossoms is said to aid anxiety, appetite loss and poor circulation. Dried hawthorn berries are used as a digestive aid in naturopathic and traditional Chinese medicine. Hawthorn is also used as an aid to lower blood pressure, and treat some heart related diseases. The haws are often used to make jams, which are considered a delicacy.

Bones, muscles and joints

Our bones, muscles and joints can be subject to injury so it is important that we look after them and take appropriate care when damage does occur. At the first sign of injury, bruising, accident or pain, take homeopathic remedy Arnica 30. This will help your body cope with the shock and also reduce swelling and ease bruising. Pain can be more acute when our bodies go into a state of shock and we forget to drink water. Dehydration makes pain worse as muscles create acidic waste when in pain. Drinking two glasses of water as soon as the pain comes on will help stop this painful waste building up and give almost immediate relief. Cold packs are also great for reducing inflammation, soothing away pain and aiding recovery – use a pack of frozen peas and press to the affected area.

The diet is also important in maintaining good muscle and joint health; essential fatty acids are great for increasing muscle flexibility and repairing muscle tissue. Make sure your diet is rich in the right kinds of fatty acids such as oily fish, hemp and flaxseed oil.

There are many plants that can be used in the treatment of aches and pains – find out how to make seaweed liniment to treat arthritis and brew up your own cider vinegar which can be used to treat a host of conditions from sprains to skin disorders, digestive upset to urinary infections.

Osteoporosis

This is when the bones lose their density with age and become more porous. Can mean that fractures and breakages in the bones are more likely. Eat plenty of calcium rich wild greens such as nettles and dandelion. The leaves of both can be made into a tea or added to soups and stews. To make a tea, simply take a handful of fresh leaves of either plant, place in a cup, add boiling water and leave to steep for ten minutes. Drink 3 cups a day if needed. Comfrey is an excellent tonic for bone health – the folk name for comfrey is in fact 'knitbone'. The leaves can be harvested in the spring and summer, and dried to make a medicinal tea.

Comfrey tea

1. Pick a bunch of comfrey leaves.
2. Tie the stems together and hang in a dry spot until the leaves have dried.
3. Cut off the stems and place the leaves in a paper bag.
4. To make a tea, take 1 tbsp dried herb and place in a cup.
5. Add boiling water, cover and allow to steep for 5 minutes.
6. Drink up to 3 cups a day.

Rheumatism

An umbrella term that covers aches, pains and stiffness in the bones and muscles. Horseradish is said to prevent attacks of rheumatism – pick a leaf and chew it slowly. Seaweed can be harvested and made into a liniment to treat rheumatism (see recipe opposite). Rose petals can be added to running water to make a soothing bath for rheumatic pain – simply add a handful and step in. A wonderful warming oil can be made from cayenne, which can be used to treat aches and pains and stiffness.

Cayenne oil

▶ I tbsp cayenne pepper
▶ 2 tbsp crushed mustard seed
▶ 2 tsp grated ginger root
▶ 250 ml (8 fl oz) sunflower oil

I. Mix all of the ingredients together in a glass jar.
2. Leave to infuse for I week.
3. Massage in to the affected area to treat muscle spasm and stiff joints.

Fractures

Often the result of injury, a fracture is a break or crack in the bone. The homeopathic remedy Arnica and a few drops of rescue remedy should be taken at the time of injury. After the injury take aloe vera internally to help

the body heal. Squeeze the juice from one leaf into a glass of warm water, or fruit juice, blend and drink. Take comfrey tea regularly after injury to help the bones to heal (see page 89). The fractured joint can also be massaged with comfrey oil (see recipe opposite), as long as the skin is not broken.

Arthritis

Inflammation of the tissues surrounding the joints. Pain, swelling and redness usually result. Nettles are a traditional remedy for arthritis and can be use in cookery or made into a tea. A glass of water with 1 tsp honey and 1 tbsp vinegar is a soothing remedy to ease the pain. Also add apple cider vinegar to a warm bath to promote healing – you can make your own by fermenting apple juice (see page 92). Make a homemade seaweed liniment to treat arthritis or rheumatism.

Seaweed liniment

▶ 25 g (1 oz) bladderwrack (from the beach)
▶ 500 ml (18 fl oz) water
▶ Comfrey oil (see right)

1. Place the bladderwrack in a saucepan and pour over the water.
2. Simmer gently for 30 minutes.
3. Strain and measure the liquid.
4. Add an equal volume of comfrey oil (see right).
5. Shake well before use. Rub into infected areas, morning and night.

Comfrey oil

▶ 1 handful of dried comfrey leaves
▶ Sweet almond oil or apricot kernel oil, enough to fill your jar

1. Place the comfrey leaves in a glass jar with a lid and cover completely with the oil.
2. Seal and leave to infuse for 4 to 8 weeks, shaking daily.
3. When the oil has turned a deeper colour, strain through a piece of muslin and pour into a dark glass bottle. Store in the refrigerator and use on its own to treat muscle pain, sprains and broken bones or add to the seaweed tonic (see left) to make a liniment.

Apple cider vinegar

Use fully ripe, unbruised apples and avoid metal utensils or containers when making or storing the vinegar as the acid will react to the metal. The amount of apples needed will depend on their size so you may need to adjust the quantities given here depending on how much juice your apples yield. This recipe is for 2 litres (3½ pints) of apple vinegar.

1. Quarter then crush the apples and strain the pulp through a piece of muslin cloth, reserving the juice.
2. To make the starter remove 250 ml (8 fl oz) of the juice and add a square of winemaker's yeast (refer to the packaging for exact quantity needed).
3. Mix thoroughly and stir into the rest of the juice.
4. Pour the mixture into a large glass bowl or lid-less container. Cover with a piece of muslin cloth and store out of direct sunlight for 3–4 weeks at a temperature of between 16°C and 26°C. Stir the mixture daily.
5. After 3 weeks taste the vinegar. If it is not strong enough, wait another week.
6. When you are happy with the flavour, strain the vinegar and pasteurize it by heating to 60°C in a saucepan .
7. Pour into clean bottles with airtight lids. Place the sealed bottles in a pan filled with hot water. Allow the water to cool and then store.

Sprains and pulled muscles

Generally the result of over stretching often caused during sports. Comfrey and arnica are affective at treating areas of damaged tissue such as a sprain. Apply an ointment or gently massage comfrey oil (see page 91) into the sore area. It is not a good idea to use either of these herbs in cases of broken skin. Make up a potent massage oil using eucalyptus, lavender and rosemary essential oils. Simply add a few drops of each of these oils to 30 ml (1½ fl oz) carrier oil, such as organic sweet almond oil and massage into the sprain twice daily. This can also be added to a hot bath to provide relief. Apple cider vinegar can be used as a cold compress on the affected limb to reduce swelling and relieve pain. You can make your own apple cider vinegar, which is also useful in the treatment of skin disorders, digestive troubles, urinary infections and illnesses of the respiratory system.

Backache

We often take our spines completely for granted until something happens to arrest their mobility. Whether caused by a fall, a bump, an awkward twist or just sheer build up of stress, pain in the back leaves us crying out for relief, and often unable to move. Most of us experience backache at some point in our lives. With an increasingly sedentary lifestyle consisting of a great deal of time spent sitting in the same position in office chairs staring at a computer screen it is hardly surprising that back pain is on the rise. Fortunately there are many ways to promote health of the spine and prevent back pain in the first place. Regular exercise is very beneficial for the health of the spine. Yoga or Pilates are particularly helping in stretching and releasing any areas of tension before they build up and become painful. Try to incorporate a daily stretching session and at least 30 minutes walking into your day. Ideally you would combine this with a session of aerobic exercise such as swimming, cycling or running. It is a good idea to aim to get your heart pumping at least once a day. Plan exercise sessions that are fun and that you can do with friends, such as a group cycle ride/walk or a dance class, which will help you to stick to them.

There are also plenty of natural remedies that can be used to treat discomfort in the back. Make up a massage oil using a base of 200 ml (7 fl oz) organic sweet almond oil with two drops each of rosemary, lavender and eucalyptus. This can be massaged into the affected area or added to a warm bath to soothe and ease pain. Chew on a small horseradish leaf to help relieve the pain. Apply a mustard poultice to the affected area to ease pain and help release blockages in the back.

Mustard poultice

▶ ½ tsp mustard seeds
▶ 1 tbsp plain flour

1. Place the mustard seeds and flour in a bowl.
2. Add enough warm water to form a paste.
3. Spread the mixture over one half of a flannel and fold the flannel over so that the poultice is covered.
4. Wear a cotton t-shirt or cover your back with a cotton sheet and place the wrapped poultice over the affected area.
5. Leave the poultice on for an hour, checking regularly that the skin hasn't become red or sore (some people have very sensitive skin and find mustard too strong). If the skin is red and uncomfortable, remove the poultice and wash with cool water.

Comfrey

Comfrey is a wonderful plant native to Europe that has a myriad of uses, not least in your garden. In fact it has been said that comfrey has more uses than any other herb. The roots can grow up to ten feet deep and draw the nutrients from deep in the soil up to ground level, into the sub soil to feed other neighbouring plants and to enrich the soil. Nutrients, minerals and moisture are transported in this way by a herb that is often grown as green manure (a plant that enriches the soil during growth and is then dug into the earth to give further nutrients at the end of the growing period) because of its beneficial effect on the soil and its usefulness as cattle feed. The plant can be recognized by its large bristly leaves and purple flower clusters in the summertime.

Some consider comfrey a weed but organic gardeners are well aware of its value. To make a nutrient-rich spray for the garden loosely fill a bucket with cut leaves and top up with water. Press down and leave for a few weeks. It will look and smells horrible but the resulting deep brown liquid can be diluted and decanted into a spray bottle to use on tomatoes, onions and beans.

Another use for comfrey in the garden is as a slug repellent. You can place cut leaves in a heap encouraging slugs to eat these instead of your new seedlings. The leaves can also be placed around the base of a plant and hopefully the slugs will feast on these before attacking your vegetables. Laurence Hills, the founder of the Henry Doubleday Research Association (now known as Garden Organic), devoted all his early work to research and experimentation with comfrey. He suggested that every organic garden should continuously have a patch of comfrey growing. Hills recommends mixing the leaves into the compost heap as an activator.

Although it has a bitter taste, comfrey is often enjoyed by humans as well as slugs and can be served in salads or steamed lightly and cooked as a green vegetable. It also makes a good base for detoxifying green drinks containing other superfoods such as spirulina. It is a rich source of Vitamin B12 and has more protein in its leaf structure than any other plant. It is an excellent detoxificant and has a cleansing effect on the liver and lung tissues. Even the root can be used to make a coffee substitute much like dandelion or chicory.

Traditional folk names for comfrey include 'knitbone' or 'boneset' due to its healing properties and use for treating broken bones by early herbalists. Today the plant is used to make an ointment that is effective in treating skin problems and bruising. Lastly the leaves can also be used to make a beautiful yellow dye. So this really is one plant that you can put to use in every area of your house and garden.

Eyes and ears

Looking after your prime sense organs is vital. There are a number of natural remedies that can be used to treat common problems with the eyes, such as conjunctivitis and eye strain. The most widely recognised herb for addressing eye problems is eyebright, or *Euphrasia officinalis*. Found throughout Europe this herb has been used since the Middle Ages to treat bloodshot and irritated eyes. The flowers, which have spots and stripes, are thought to resemble bloodshot eyes, and followers of the Doctrine of Signatures believe that plants exhibit signs of the symptoms they can be used to treat. On the following pages you can learn how to make an eye brightening infusion, which can be used to treat conjunctivitis, styes and eyestrain.

Modern lifestyles often involve spending a great deal of time in front of a computer screen or focusing on objects close to us, causing our eyes to suffer from tiredness. Make sure that they get adequate rest and also that you spend time every day looking into the distance. Our ancestors would have spent much of their time watching the horizon and looking at things far away. It is thought that increasing levels of myopia (or short-sightedness) are in part caused by our tendency to focus on the small things in front of us. It is a good idea to take a 15 minute walk every day and really focus on the horizon while you are walking. You can also try an eye yoga exercise to relieve tired eyes. Rub your palms together vigorously to create heat, then place your palms over your eyes for several minutes and breathe deeply.

The ears are prone to infection when there is a build up of mucous in the system, and this can be treated using garlic and raw onion. Another traditional remedy for the ears is mullein, a beautiful tall plant with a spike of big blousy flowers. In this chapter you'll find out how to make your own mullein oil, which can be used to treat infection and build up of wax.

Conjunctivitis

Inflammation of the mucous membrane that lines the eyelids and covers the outer layer of the eyeball. It can be a reaction to allergens in the atmosphere, such as pollens, or cosmetics. Dilute a tablespoon of honey in a cup of warm water to make an eye bath that will cleanse the area, treat an infection and promote healing. Make an eye wash using a cup of tepid camomile tea. A cotton pad can be used to cleanse the eye. Make sure that you use a new pad for each eye to reduce the risk of spreading the infection. Lavender, camomile or rose essential oil can be added to warm water to make a soothing eye bath that will draw out the infection.

Eyebright infusion

Use infusion of eyebright to help restore health to itchy, infected eyes.

1. Soak 4 mg of dried eyebright in a cup of boiled water for 10 minutes.
2. Strain and cool.
3. Using a clean flannel bathe the eyes with this infusion twice daily.

Styes

Small yellow blister at the base of the eyelash that occur when the immune system is compromised. See remedies for Conjunctivitis on page 97 to soothe any irritation. A calendula tincture can also be applied topically to reduce swelling and taken internally to support the immune system. Dilute 1 tbsp tincture to a cup of warm water and drink up to three times a day.

Calendula tincture

▶ A large handful of fresh calendula flowers
▶ 200 ml (7 fl oz) alcohol (such as organic vodka)
▶ 100 ml (3½ fl oz) water

1. Place the flowers in a large glass jar.
2. Cover with the alcohol and water.
3. Replace the lid and leave for 2 weeks, shaking occasionally.
4. Strain through a sieve with a muslin cloth places inside.
5. Pour the liquid into a clean dark glass bottle and store for up to a year.

Eyestrain

After staring at a screen for several hours your eyes can become tired and feel irritated. Add 2 drops of rose essential oil to 2 tablespoons carrier oil, such as organic olive oil, and massage into the temples to relieve tension.

Chickweed infusion

1. Place a handful of chickweed leaves into a teapot.
2. Add 2 cups of boiling water.
3. Leave for 10 minutes then strain.
4. Soak a cloth in the liquid, fold into a rectangle and rest over the eyes for 10 minutes.

You can also make an infusion using rose petals. Place a handful in a cup of boiling water, cover and leave to infuse for ten minutes. Strain and then use the liquid to bathe the eyes. Place slices of cucumber over the eyes to calm and soothe the eye area. Make a compress from an infusion of chickweed to ease tired sore eyes.

Middle ear infection

An ear infection is sometimes a side-effect of a sore throat or chesty cold, often accompanied by fever. Use garlic extensively in the diet to help the body rid itself of infection. You can also place a piece of cut, peeled garlic wrapped in gauze directly into the ear to treat the infection. Naturopaths often recommend a slice of raw onion placed around the ear to draw out infection. Leave it in place for as long as possible and replace when it has dried out.

Take several pieces of yarrow and cover with boiling water. Leave for 10 minutes then pour the still warm infusion into the ear to help reduce infection. Massage lavender oil into the neck and throat area. Mullein is the herbal remedy for ears and you can make an effective oil from this plant. Drop a pipette full into your ear canal and keep your head on one side to absorb.

Mullein oil

1. Break the flowering spike of a mullein plant into smaller pieces.
2. Place in a pestle and add a small amount of organic sunflower oil.
3. Crush with the mortar to start releasing the beneficial parts of the plant.
4. Place in a large glass jar.
5. Cover with more oil so that the plant is well covered then put the lid on and shake well
6. Leave outside in direct sunlight for 21 days.

Ear wax build up

Hard wax sometimes accumulates in the ear and an excess can obstruct the canal and affect hearing. This condition can be made worse by swimming as the wax absorbs water. Warm some mullein oil and place a few drops into the ear canal.

Fennel

Fennel (*Foeniculum vulgare*) is a perennial and umbelliferous plant, meaning that it has umbrella-like bursts of flowers on tall, upright stalks. The common garden fennel has soft, feathery foliage which smells of aniseed when crushed, and it looks very similar to the dill plant. The species Florence fennel possesses the swollen, bulb-like stem base, which is the familiar vegetable most often using in cooking. The thin, ovoid, grooved seeds are used extensively for their sweet, aniseed flavour. Fennel is indigenous to Europe but cultivated in India, China and Egypt.

Fennel's rich and interesting history is chronicled in herbal folklore. The Ancient Greeks valued fennel highly – one of their most famous cities, Marathon (which translates as 'fennel') was so named because of the abundance of the aromatic herb growing there. The Romans cultivated the plant for its edible shoots and seeds and recorded its use to sharpen the sight of snakes. Mediaeval English herbalists prized it for many reasons, including its professed power to ward away evil. Fennel features in the pagan Anglo-Saxon Nine Herbs Charm, recorded in the 10th century. This fascinating charm was intended for the treatment of poison and infection through the preparation of nine herbs.

Fennel crops up in the culinary traditions of many different cultures. The bulb of Florence fennel is popular in Mediterranean countries where it features in salads, pastas and risottos, along with the tasty fronds. The Chinese use fennel in their five-spice powder and the seeds are an integral part of the flavours of many Indian and Middle Eastern dishes.

As a medicinal herb, fennel is perhaps best known for its digestive carminative properties. Try bruising a teaspoon of fennel seeds and adding boiling water to make a soothing and antispasmodic tea. This creates an excellent tonic to ease bloating, indigestion and flatulence. Fennel was traditionally mixed with sodium bicarbonate and syrup to make gripe water, given to babies to ease painful colic. As far back as the Ancient Greeks, fennel was used as a slimming aid as it can suppress the appetite.

Fennel has a long history of use for the treatment of eye problems and on the Indian subcontinent fennel seeds are often eaten raw to improve eyesight. A fennel compress can help with conjunctivitis and blepharitis. As a folk remedy, fennel has been used for jaundice, hepatitis and other liver disorders as it is said to restore damaged liver cells. To help cleanse the liver drink a tea made with one teaspoon of bruised fennel seed or two teaspoons of finely chopped fresh leaves to a cup of boiling water.

Breast-feeding mothers find the gifts of fennel to be manifold. It works as a galactogogue, improving milk flow in a gentle and safe way. A cooling compress made with bruised fennel seeds can be used for engorged and painful breasts. The plant contains phytoestrogens – plant compounds that exert a balancing effect on female hormone levels. This makes it an ideal companion throughout life and many women find it very helpful for hormonal upsets ranging from PMT to the menopause. There is reported use of fennel to enlarge the breasts dating back to Roman times when it was also used to increase the libido. Although there are no guarantees, drinking fennel tea is a far more holistic option than surgery!

Women's health

As women, we are blessed with amazing bodies that follow the cycles of the moon in our menstruation, have the ability to carry, nurture and give birth to babies and then provide the perfect nutrients in the form of breast milk for our children. In our medicalized society it is possible to forget the power and strength of our bodies. We may take medication to control the menstrual period or even eliminate it altogether. When pregnant, we often forget to trust our instincts and listen to what our bodies need and may not take time marvel at the miracle happening inside us, and when labour kicks in most doctors and midwives advise the mother to go to the hospital to be helped to give birth.

This is the norm in our society but many women are starting to question it and look outside the mainstream for alternatives. Of course medical help is an essential part of giving birth and modern medicine can aid the various hormonal transitions women go through, but nature also offers us a wealth of ways to help with these natural processes. When we can embrace our monthly bleeding and the possible emotions that come up with it, rather than trying to control it, we may find that the strain and pain is lessened. When we can trust our innate ability to birth and nurture our young, working with our bodies as nature intended, we can re-discover the amazing power we have to create new life. This section is all about women's bodies and ways to treat our life processes such as periods, pregnancy, birth and the menopause naturally.

Menstrual cycle

Since ancient times it has been believed that menstrual cycles are connected to the moon, causing women to bleed at the dark (or new) moon and ovulate when the moon is full. Many women have problems with their menstrual cycle but there are a host of natural remedies that can be used to create a balance.

Dysmenorrhoea is the name given to painful periods, while menorrhagia means heavy bleeding and the absence of periods is known as amenorrhea. Many of us suffer with period pain every month and this could, in part, be due to our culture. Periods are often seen as something shameful, to be hidden and to be suffered. It is not often that we allow ourselves to rest and take time out during our monthly bleed, although this is practiced by some tribal cultures around the world even today. While the demands of modern life may not allow us complete rest, even in today's fast-paced society we can incorporate a time of relaxation into our everyday lives. Promise yourself an afternoon in bed, a lie-in or an early night at the start of your period. Indulge your taste buds – what would you like to eat now? Treat yourself and let go of guilt. Make your own comfort you maximum priority – are you warm enough? Do you need an extra blanket? More pillows? Would you like a hot water bottle placed on your abdomen or lower back? It may be helpful to mark when your cycle begins on a calender or in a diary and note how you feel each day, remembering that self-care during this time of the month is vital. Once you get into the flow of this you may start to notice an easing of your usual symptoms.

Peppermint tea can help to ease bloating and pain during menstruation. Make a massage oil with a few drops each of clary sage and fennel essential oil added to 30 ml (1½ fl oz) carrier oil. Massage into the abdomen and lower back to regulate the hormones.

Fertility

Fertility has become a subject of huge anxiety for many women throughout the Western world. But the impulse to turn to drugs and invasive medical procedures is in many cases unnecessary. Alternative therapies have been found to be extremely effective in correcting and restoring full reproductive function. Firstly, diet is extremely important in reproductive health. Vitamin C, selenium and zinc are particularly important. Zinc is critical for maintaining optimum levels of semen, and essential for the functioning of male and female reproductive organs – it is also one of the minerals most depleted by sustained stress levels and toxic lifestyles. Vitamin C is important in sperm production, as it improves mobility. Selenium deficiencies have been linked to reduced sperm counts and sterility in men and infertility in women. This mineral can be found in Brazil nuts so ensure that these tasty nuts are a regular part of your diet.

Cutting down on toxins will boost vitality, libido and fertility. Alcohol and tobacco are known to reduce sperm count and can prevent implantation of the fertilized egg in women. Fried, fatty foods, sugar and caffeine should be limited or eliminated if possible. A diet high in essential fatty acids (found in flax, hemp, oily fish, pumpkin seeds) has been shown to be beneficial.

Pregnancy

Pregnancy is the start of the parenting journey. It is an incredible period of creativity and change during which it is important to nurture both body and mind. A woman's body is often optimally healthy during pregnancy and this state of health can be encouraged through a good diet and holistic therapies. There is a natural tendency for self-healing when minor illnesses or imbalances occur. Natural therapies can work with the body to enhance and strengthen this ability. If used appropriately, most alternative medicines have no dangerous or unpleasant side effects and are safe for use in pregnancy, however some herbs and herbal remedies are best avoided during pregnancy. If you are in any doubt always check with a trained herbalist or doctor.

Anaemia

Low iron levels in the blood can cause feelings of weakness, dizziness and fainting. Take red raspberry leaf tea, which contains iron that is easily assimilated into the system. This is best avoided until the final trimester however, as raspberry can cause the uterus to contract. When eating foods containing iron, such as watercress, pumpkin seeds and oats, remember that vitamin C, found in many fruits and green vegetables, is needed by the body to break down the iron. Also see page 84.

Backache

Can be caused by changes in your posture needed to accommodate the baby's weight. Try to stand straight and tall and wear comfortable shoes. Yoga and pilates can be very beneficial in helping to encourage a better posture. Poses such as Cat stretch and Two Foot Support can help you to really become aware of the spine and its correct alignment, but be aware that not all poses are suitable for pregnant women.

Soothing massage oil

A good massage oil for backache during pregnancy and a useful tool for easing aches and pains.

▶ 2 drops each of rose, geranium, lavender and roman Camomile essential oils
▶ 30 ml (1½ fl oz) sweet almond oil

1. Drop the essential oils into a glass jar.
2. Add the sweet almond oil and shake to mix. Use as a massage treatment or add a capful to warm running water for a soothing bath.

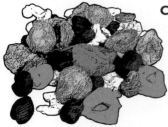

Constipation

Difficulty in passing stools sometimes caused by over-the-counter iron supplements. Cut back on wheat products, eat more dried fruits and take more fluids. As some prescription iron supplements can have a constipating effect, try an iron-rich tonic such as Floradix or make yourself some nettle tea, which is naturally rich in iron.

Bleeding gums

Hormonal changes can lead to a softening of the gum tissue, which is more easily damaged during pregnancy. Increase your Vitamin C intake to help your body heal and to strengthen the gums. Red raspberry leaf tea is also good for treating bleeding gums, but limit the use of this herb to the third trimester.

Cramps

During pregnancy, cramps occur mainly in the thighs, calves and feet due to poor circulation or calcium deficiency. Eat plenty of garlic to improve circulation. A daily leg massage also helps prevent cramping at night. See page 105 for a soothing massage oil blend.

Fluid retention

The balance of salt and potassium in the cells causes hands, legs and feet to swell. Massage can help to reduce water retention in the legs – try the massage oil blend on page 105.

Dizziness

Change position slowly so that your blood vessels have time to adjust and eat little and often.

Indigestion

Abdominal discomfort due to reduced capacity to digest food. Drink fennel tea and avoid rich, spicy or fried foods. Yoga and pilates can alleviate the pain caused by pressure on the diaphragm.

Fennel tea

1. Take 1 tbsp dried fennel seeds and place in a cup.
2. Pour boiling water over to cover.
3. Place a plate on top to allow to infuse for ten minutes.
4. Drink after a meal to help the body digest more easily.

Insomnia

Discomfort near the end of pregnancy can make sleeping difficult. A teaspoon of honey and cider vinegar in warm water can help you get more restful sleep. Also try drinking celery juice. Daily exercise, preferably outdoors, is a real tonic for sleeplessness. Try a barefoot walk on the lawn before bed. It may sound silly but it helps to discharge the electromagnetic charge that builds up during the day and helps to promote restful sleep. Take little naps during the day and avoid watching TV before you go to bed. In fact switch off any electrical equipment at the wall. Also, make sure your bedroom is well ventilated.

Morning sickness

A feeling of nausea usually experienced in the first three months of pregnancy. Severe morning sickness may cause regular vomiting and is not necessarily confined to the morning. Ginger is very good for nausea. Try making a cup of ginger tea by steeping fresh ginger in hot water for ten minutes. Try homeopathic remedies – Ipecac for continued nausea not relieved by vomiting; Sepia if the nausea is made worse by the smell or thought of food; Nux Vomica for nausea that is worse in the morning; and Pulsatilla for nausea that comes on in the evening. When you have to travel long distances when pregnant wear a pair of travel bands on your wrists which work on acupressure points and are available from most good health food stores or chemists. Boost your levels of Vitamin B6, found in bananas, cereals, lentils and fish.

Pelvic pain
Pain in the pelvis caused by pressure on the pelvic nerves. Massage the thighs and pelvic area quite firmly to relieve muscle pain and tightness. See page 105 for a massage oil recipe.

Haemorrhoids
Caused by a body under stress through lack of nutrients. Apply an ice-cold witch hazel compress (see page 85) on gauze over the swelling. Also see page 85.

Stretch marks
Fine red lines that eventually turn silver, caused by the skin stretching. Apply aloe vera gel direct from the succulent leaves onto your belly, breasts and thighs to prevent stretch marks. Food containing zinc, such as sunflower and pumpkin seeds, can help to boost your skin's elasticity.

Growing bump oil

Try moisturizing your growing bump with this coconut and rose oil to help prevent stretch marks.

▶ 100 ml (3½ fl oz) coconut oil
▶ 5 drops rose essential oil

1. Place the coconut oil and rose essential oil into a small glass bowl.
2. Warm slightly over a pan of boiling water.
3. Massage the warm, sweetly scented oil into your abdomen.

Thrush

This vaginal infection is often caused by extra pressure on the immune system during pregnancy. Camomile, fennel and thyme can be used to treat thrush with their anti-fungal properties. Make an infusion by adding 1 tablespoon of each dried herb to a bowl of boiling water. Cover and allow to infuse for 10 minutes. Strain and soak a cloth in the tepid water. Apply as a compress to the vagina. Natural yogurt can also be applied. Eat plenty of raw foods, especially garlic. You can also massage olive oil liberally around the vulva and labia. Wear cotton underwear and avoid tight fitting clothes. Cut out sugar and other sweeteners such as honey and molasses, as sugar distresses the immune system.

Tiredness

Your body is creating a new human being – it is understandable that you will feel more tired than usual. Try and make time to rest several times a day and ensure that you get adequate sleep by having early nights when possible. Have a warm bath with a few drops of jasmine, ylang ylang or lavender oil to help relax the body ready for sleep. Yoga and swimming are perfect exercise for pregnancy and can energise you when you are feeling exhausted. They will also ensure a good night's sleep.

Childbirth

Practicing yoga during pregnancy can have an amazing effect on the body's ability to open up to childbirth. Practicing the squat position is especially good for the pelvic region. An active birth, when you move around during childbirth and are able to give birth in an upright or all fours position, rather than lying flat on your back, works with rather than against gravity.

When pregnant it is a good idea to make up a natural birth toolkit to use during labour containing the natural remedies that can be used to ease the contractions and to help the body to heal afterwards. Below are some items you might like to include in your natural birth kit.

• A massage oil made with a few drops each of essential oils of clary sage and rose, added to 30 ml (1½ fl oz) base oil, such as organic sweet almond oil. Ask your midwife or partner to rub this into your lower back.
• Lavender and melissa essential oils, both of which can be applied to a handkerchief and inhaled to help you stay focussed and used as a pick-me-up if you are feeling overwhelmed.
• Rescue Remedy, which can be taken for anxiety during labour and immediately after the birth to help the body begin the healing process. Add five drops to a glass of water and take small sips.
• A jar of honey to keep your strength up – a teaspoon can be taken as required.
• Red raspberry leaf tea can be drunk to help get labour started.
• Camomile tea is useful in cases of anxiety or shaking.

Breast feeding

A mother's milk is the perfect food for her baby. It contains all the essential nutrients and changes throughout development to provide exactly what the child needs at each stage. The first milk is called colostrum, a thick yellow milk that has high immune boosting properties, especially important in the first days after the baby leaves the womb. The milk, which arrives around three days after birth, contains higher levels of proteins and fats to promote growth. A mother's milk continues to change to support the growing child and when a baby starts to eat solid food, the mother's breast milk adapts to provide more antibodies to protect the child's digestive system. In addition to the essential nutrients and immune boosting properties that breast milk offers, the act of breast feeding is an important way to bond with a new baby. Skin-to-skin contact is vital for healthy development and breast feeding encourages production of the nurturing hormone, prolactin. There are natural remedies that you can take to increase milk flow and to help heal sore nipples.

Milk production

The more a baby feeds the more milk is produced, so an easy way to increase production is to feed your baby more frequently to get a good supply established. Fennel tea can also be taken to boost milk production.

Sore, cracked nipples

A little expressed breast milk massaged into the affected area can help to heal cracked nipples. This condition can be very painful but try to keep milk the flowing to prevent engorgement. If it is too uncomfortable to breast feed on the affected breast, gently express milk by hand. Calendula salve can soothe sore skin and promotes healing. It is safe for babies to swallow.

Problems with let-down

Breast feeding is most effective when mother and baby are relaxed. If you are having problems relaxing, try having a warm bath with a few drops of lavender essential oil or make up a bottle of your own soothing milk flow bath oil. Try feeding your baby in the bath – you may find that the warm water helps them relax too.

Milk boosting drink

1. Steep 25 g (1 oz) fennel seeds in a cup of boiling water.
2. Leave to infuse for ten minutes, strain and then drink whilst still warm.
3. Take up to three times a day.

Calendula salve

▶ 250 ml (8 fl oz) calendula oil (see page 76)
▶ 50 g (2 oz) beeswax
▶ A few drops of rose essential oil

1. Melt the beeswax in a glass bowl over a pan of hot water.
2. Add the calendula oil and rose essential oil.
3. Mix thoroughly and pour into a dark glass jar with a tight fitting lid. Storing in the refrigerator and apply to sore nipples to help them heal.

Milk flow bath oil

▶ 2 drops each of lavender, ylang ylang and roman Camomile essential oils
▶ 30 ml (1½ fl oz) organic sweet almond oil

1. Drop the essential oils into a glass jar and add the sweet almond oil.
2. Shake to mix and add a capful to warm water for a soothing bath.

Engorgement

During the first weeks after birth your breasts can become full and hard. Feeding frequently should bring relief. Leaves from a Savoy cabbage kept cool in the refrigerator can be applied to the breasts to reduce swelling and absorb heat.

Inflammation

Savoy cabbage leaves can be tucked inside your bra to calm inflammation. Echinacea tincture taken in a glass of water will help the body to fight infection. Calendula and camomile essential oils are anti-inflammatory and can be diluted in a carrier oil, such as sweet almond, and massaged into your breasts.

Soothing breast oil

▶ 2 drops each of calendula and camomile essential oils
▶ 30 ml (1½ fl oz) sweet almond oil

1. Drop the essential oils into a glass jar and add the sweet almond oil.
2. Shake to mix and gently massage into the breasts.

Tiredness

Rest when your baby is resting. Once breastfeeding is established you might find it comfortable to lie down on your side and rest whilst your baby is feeding. Ensure you are eating plenty of energy-rich foods and drinking lots of fluids to keep your energy levels up. Try slow-releasing energy foods such as oats, nuts, seeds, sprouts and bananas.

Menopause

This marks the end of menstruation, which happens at around the age of 50. There can be disorientating side effects such as hot flushes and memory loss. Clary sage is a great mood enhancer and also balances the hormones. Place a few drops on to a handkerchief and inhale as required throughout the day. To reduce the incidence of night sweats, take a bath with camomile essential oil before bed. Simply add a few drops to a warm bath.

Ensure that you get plenty of magnesium in the diet – nettles are a rich source and are available free on our doorsteps. Forget about expensive supplements and make yourself a nourishing nettle tonic. Don't worry about stings – the histamine is no longer active after the leaves have been boiled or blended.

Nettle tonic

1. Place several handfuls of nettle tops in a large saucepan
2. Cover with boiling water.
3. Boil for 30 minutes.
4. Strain through a muslin cloth and drink as required.

Menopause tea

Motherwort is a traditional remedy for helping ease the body through the transition. Drink motherwort tea as often as needed.

1. Steep 25 g (1 oz) dried motherwort in a cup of boiling water.
2. Leave to infuse for 10 minutes, strain and then drink whilst still warm.

Motherwort

Motherwort has been an important herb since Roman times. The Latin name, *Leonurus cardiaca*, is derived from the Greek word meaning 'lion-hearted'. The ancient Greeks used motherwort to relieve anxiety in mothers after childbirth. It really is a women's herb, being valuable in the treatment of menstruation and menopausal problems as well as after childbirth. It is a member of the mint family, has a square stem and opposite leaves. Small pink and lilac flowers appear on the upper part of the plant in summer. The plant grows to about a metre/yard in height and can be found along roadsides and in vacant fields and other waste areas.

Today, motherwort is used to stimulate delayed or suppressed periods and to ease the discomfort of dysmenorrhoea (painful menstruation). The plant contains constituents that act as a gentle uterine stimulant. It is for this reason that it should not be used in pregnancy although after childbirth it helps to restore the uterus and to reduce the risk of bleeding after birth (postpartum haemorrhage).

Motherwort can be used during the menopausal years to treat hot flushes, fainting, stressed nerves and sleep disorders. For hot flushes add a few drops of tincture to a small glass of water and drink to harness the herb's great relaxative properties.

Used regularly, motherwort feeds your nerves and your good common sense, relaxing and unclenching any held tension. Motherwort is not sedating but calming, leaving you ready for action, not flying off the handle or bouncing off the walls. Motherwort is your ally in tough times, and 10 to 20 drops of tincture taken as soon as you feel your nerves starting to fray or just before a stressful event can have a wonderfully calming effect. This can be repeated every five minutes if needed.

Heart conditions are also treated with this common herb, hence *cardiaca* in the Latin name. It invigorates the circulation and increases oxygen in the blood. Motherwort calms a rapidly beating heart with readily usable minerals, trace elements and an alkaloid exceptionally tonifying to the heart (and uterus). The German herbal doctor, Weiss, uses motherwort tincture for those with functional heart complaints. A dropperful of motherwort tincture acts quickly to ease palpitations and tachycardia (heart rate disorders). Regular use lowers hypertension, and sets you up to be a hale-hearted elder.

At night motherwort's high-calcium calming effect can be put to good use when you are awakened and have difficulty getting back to sleep. Keep a glass of water and a bottle of motherwort tincture by your bed and take 10 to 15 drops and a mouthful of water as soon as you wake.

Sweet violet

Sweet violet (*viola odorata*) is an evergreen perennial. Although the plants are in leaf all year, it flowers from early spring. It is often found in areas of semi-shade such as woodland and grassy verges. In the kitchen, the leaves and flowers of sweet violet can be a welcome reminder of the warmer days to come. The flowers can be used as a colourful yet delicately flavoured addition to a salad, or as a decoration for cakes and puddings. Young leaves have a mild flavour, although they can become quite tough as they grow older. If you can find fresh, young leaves, they make a very good salad; their mild flavour enabling them to be used in bulk. When added to soup they thicken in a similar way to okra. A soothing tea can be made from the leaves and flowers. For medicinal purposes, sweet violet has a long and proven history of folk use, especially in the treatment of cancer and whooping cough. It also contains salicylic acid, which is used to make aspirin. It is therefore effective in the treatment of headaches, migraine and insomnia. The whole plant is anti-inflammatory, diaphoretic, diuretic, emollient, expectorant and laxative. It is taken internally in the treatment of bronchitis, respiratory catarrh, coughs, asthma, and cancer of the breast, lungs or digestive tract.

Externally, it is used to treat mouth and throat infections. The plant can either be used fresh, or harvested when it comes into flower and then dried for later use. The flowers are demulcent and emollient, and are used in the treatment of biliousness and lung troubles. The petals can be made into a syrup and used in the treatment of childhood illnesses, such as whooping cough. The roots are a much stronger expectorant than other parts of the plant but they also contain the alkaloid, violine, which at higher doses can be strongly purgative, causing diarrhoea and vomiting. They are usually gathered in the autumn and dried for later use.

A homeopathic remedy is made from the whole fresh plant, which is considered useful in the treatment of spasmodic coughs and rheumatism of the wrist. An essential oil from the flowers is used in aromatherapy in the treatment of bronchial complaints, exhaustion and skin complaints.

Plants can be grown as an effective weed-excluding ground cover when spaced about 30 cm (11¾ in) apart. Sweet violet succeeds in most soils but prefers a cool, moist, well-drained humus-rich soil in partial or dappled shade and protection from winds. When grown in the open it prefers a moderately heavy rich soil. Sweet violets are very ornamental plants and there are many named varieties. They produce their delicately scented flowers in late winter and early spring – these are designed for fertilization by bees and since there are few bees around at this time of year these flowers seldom set seed. However, the plants also produce a second type of flower later in the year. These never open, but seed is produced within them by self-fertilization. The plants will spread fairly rapidly at the roots when they are growing well.

Most members of this genus have edible leaves and flower buds, although those species with yellow flowers can cause diarrhoea if eaten in large quantities. Seed is best sown in the autumn in a cold frame. The seed requires a period of cold stratification and the germination of stored seed can be erratic. Prick out the seedlings into individual pots when they are large enough to handle and plant them out in the summer. Divide in the autumn or just after flowering. Larger divisions can be planted out direct into their permanent positions. Plant out in the summer or the following spring.

Babies and children

Using natural medicine is a gentle and rewarding approach to your family's health. Supporting and nurturing a child through an illness, whether it be a cold or chicken pox, can have a beneficial physiological effect on parent and child. Rather than resorting to pain-blocking over-the-counter drugs, treating the illness naturally aids the immune system and allows the body to fight the infection, making room for the developmental leap that often takes place after a period of convalescing.

In addition, holistic medicine treats the whole person rather than just the symptoms as in allopathic medicine. For example, a child with a cough and a sore throat is likely to be prescribed a cough suppressant and antibiotics by his doctor, in order to treat their symptoms. A homeopath treating the same child will consult with the parent and, if appropriate, the child, in an effort to discover the child's general state of health and characteristics before providing a remedy that best treats the whole child – his mind, body and soul. Other holistic therapies work in the same way, treating the person, and not just the symptoms he or she is exhibiting.

The most important advice when treating children is to listen to them. Children have an amazing self-preservation instinct and often know exactly what they need to get better. Some children stop eating when they are ill, as their bodies need to concentrate on getting well rather than using precious energy to digest food. Other children crave specific foods or can tell you exactly what what they need to feel better.

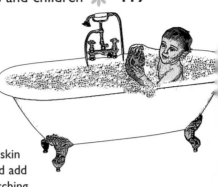

Chickenpox

Common viral infection, which causes a rash across the body – small red raised spots that develop into inflamed blisters – fever and headache. Ensure plenty of rest and fluids. The homeopathic remedy Rhus Tox will soothe the skin irritation. Sponge the body with tepid water and add bicarbonate of soda to the bathwater to ease itching.

Coughs

This is nature's way of clearing an infection of the bronchial passages and protecting the lungs from damage. For this reason, do not suppress a cough. The homeopathic remedy Bryonia is effective at treating coughs and is available in pilule or syrup form. Echinacea boosts the immune system. A hot honey and lemon drink can be drunk as often as required. Place a teaspoon of honey and the juice of half a lemon in a cup, fill with boiling water, and allow to cool before drinking. Also see page 64.

Colds

This is a natural purification process. If you discourage or suppress it could carry on in another form for many months. Get rest and drink plenty of fluids. Pulsatilla, the homeopathic remedy is effective at treating colds with mucus. Ensure plenty of onions and garlic in the diet. A honey and lemon drink soothes and cleanses. A cup of ginger tea can be soothing and warming to the system.

Ginger tea

1. Grate a small piece of root ginger into a cup of boiling water
2. Cover and leave for 10 minutes.
3. Strain before serving and add 1 tsp honey and 1 tbsp lemon juice to boost the healing properties, if desired.

Croup

Acute inflammation and narrowing of the airways, which causes wheezing and whistling breathing and a barking cough. Spongia is the homeopathic remedy for croup. Steam inhalation can ease breathing.

Earache

Discomfort in the ear due to build up of mucus. This can also be a symptom mumps – if you suspect this is the case, see page 123 for advice. A hot-water bottle placed over the ear can soothe the pain. Mullein oil, diluted in a carrier oil, can be dropped into the ear to ease discomfort.

Eczema

When the body cannot eliminate toxins through the usual channels, being the lungs, kidneys or liver, the body expels them through the skin. Skin problems such as eczema are the result – a hot itchy rash that is usually found behind the knees, on the hands, feet and behind the ears. Avoid petroleum-based

Steam inhaler

1. Place 2 drops of lavender or Camomile essential oil in a large bowl of boiling water
2. Encourage your child to lean over and inhale the steam.

For babies and small children, take them into the bathroom and turn the shower on. The hot water will create steam in the room, which will aid your child's breathing.

Ear drops

1. Break the flowering spike of a mullein plant into smaller pieces.
2. Place in a pestle and add a small amount of organic sunflower oil.
3. Crush with the mortar to start releasing the beneficial parts of the plant.
4. Place in a large glass jar. Cover with more oil so that the plant is well covered then put the lid on and shake well
5. Leave outside in direct sunlight for 21 days.
6. Strain and bottle in a dark bottle.
7. Add 1 tsp of this oil to 30 ml (1½ fl oz) of carrier oil, such as organic sweet almond oil.
8. Use a pipette to apply three drops to each ear.

products, soaps and scented baby products and do not use detergents or fabric softeners to wash the family's clothes. Diet can sometimes be the cause. With the help of a nutritionist, try eliminating dairy products from your child's diet and also the mother's if breast feeding. An oat bath (see page 69) will soothe inflamed skin before bed and visualisation can also be beneficial for a good night's sleep. Choose organic cotton clothing, especially for those items worn next to the skin, such as babygrows and underwear. Also see page 69.

Fever

This is nature's most efficient healing tool. A fever is the body's mechanism for burning up unwanted matter to combat infection. A high temperature is to be encouraged as it is cleaning out the body. However, it is vital to consult a doctor if your newborn baby is running a high temperature or if your child has ingested a poisonous substance. A dry fever is dangerous but a wet fever heals. Keep your child's fluid intake as

Rehydration drink

▶ I tbsp sugar
▶ I tbsp salt
▶ 500 ml (18 fl oz) filtered water
▶ I litre (1¾ pint) fresh apple juice

1. Place the sugar and salt in a jug.
2. Add the water and apple juice.
3. Encourage your child to drink throughout the day.

high as possible – make sure that you have drinks that they like available. A rehydration drink can aid your child's recovery after diarrhoea, vomiting or during a fever. If breast feeding, allow them to feed for as long and as often as they need. If your child is refusing to drink, run a warm bath. Sponge with tepid water afterwards and dress your child in one thin cotton layer. Keep the environment well ventilated. Your child may choose not to eat during the fever, but this is perfectly normal. Encourage them to eat once the fever has passed.

Head lice

An infestation of parasites that live one the scalp and in the hair. Can be very pervasive and tricky to get rid of. The most effective treatment is regularly brushing with a fine comb. Avoid the chemical-based products available in pharmacies, as these often contain powerful insecticides. Instead use a herbal treatment to deter and remove head lice.

Herbal head lice treatment

▶ 5 drops each of tea tree, eucalyptus, rosemary and lavender essential oil
▶ 100 ml of sweet almond oil

1. Combine the essential oils with the sweet almond oil.
2. Rub into the child's hair and leave for 12 hours.
3. Wash out and comb thoroughly.

Measles

Infectious disease caused by a virus that begins like a cold, followed by a fever, which is accompanied by a rash. Flat brown red spots usually come out on the ears and face. Lymph nodes will swell and your child is likely to feel extremely unwell. Vomiting and diarrhoea can also be symptoms. Ensure time for the child to rest and recuperate. Hot honey and lemon drinks are soothing and will help the body to heal. Add a few drops of lavender oil to cool water and sponge down. Also see fever on page 121.

Nappy rash

A sore itchy rash caused by wearing nappies. Refrain from using perfumed wipes, which can be a harsh irritant to delicate skin. Use a cotton flannel soaked in warm water instead. Allow plenty of nappy-free time, and apply calendula ointment to soothe sore skin.

Sore throat and coughs

Usually caused by an infection in the upper respiratory tract, can also be the symptoms of many other illnesses. Sage or thyme tea can be made with honey to soothe a sore throat. The homeopathic remedy Heper Sulph. can be used. Onions are a traditional remedy for soothing sore throats and easing coughs. Make your own cough medicine using the healing powers of honey and raw onion.

> ### Cough medicine
>
> This makes an effective syrup for sore throats, coughs and colds.
>
> 1. Place half an onion cut into rings into a shallow dish.
> 2. Cover with honey and leave to infuse overnight.
> 3. In the morning, strain and bottle the resulting liquid.

Teething

The homeopathic remedies Chamomilla and Pulsatilla are recommended. Camomile tea can also be helpful to ease the discomfort of new teeth coming through. Amber worn as a necklace is a natural analgesic to ease pain in the mouth. Wear a string of amber beads (available from natural babycare shops) to ease teething discomfort.

Mumps

A viral infection which causes fever and swelling of the lymph glands in the neck. Camomile tea can be cooling and soothing to the system. Make a teapot of Camomile tea and pour a cup for your child. Allow the rest to cool, soak a cloth in the liquid and then use to sponge and cool down the body. Cleavers (or sticky weed) is a cleansing herb for treating the mumps infection.

> ### Cleaver infusion
>
> 1. Gather a handful of cleavers, chop up and add to a cup.
> 2. Cover with boiling water.
> 3. Leave to infuse for 10 minutes.
> 4. Drink a cup a day whilst infection persists.

Camomile

Camomile is one of nature's most healing and soothing plants, and has had a medicinal reputation in Europe for over 2000 years. Plants have feathery green leaves and delicate daisy-like flowers which, when crushed, give off a faint scent reminiscent of apples. It is this characteristic that led to the plant being called 'ground-apple' by the Greeks – 'kamai' meaning on the ground and 'melon' meaning an apple. The Spanish call camomile 'Manzanilla,' which translates as 'a little apple,' and give the same name to one of their lightest sherries, flavoured with this plant. The Egyptians held this herb in the same high regard, and dedicated it to their gods because of its power to cure ague.

It has been grown for centuries in domestic gardens, both as an excellent companion crop and for the many health benefits it offers. In the Middle Ages it was used as a strewing herb because of its lovely, pungent smell, and was planted in lawns as the scent is aroused through walking upon the plant. It has been called the 'plant's physician' and some gardeners believe that if another plant is drooping or sickly it will recover if you place a camomile plant near it. It is reputed to enhance the growth of cucumbers and onions if planted nearby.

Most are familiar with the refreshing taste of a cup of camomile tea. An infusion of camomile is an ideal way to relax and unwind. Studies have shown that the herb is an effective mild sedative and for this reason, is a great help in cases of insomnia. In cases of severe diarrhoea, the soothing properties of camomile come to the fore and an infusion can be sipped to ease painful stomach ache and digestion. It relieves the vomiting caused by gastritis as well as heartburn. Camomile is often used to help anorexia sufferers, as it improves the appetite. Herbalists have long relied upon camomile as a herb to relieve menstrual cramps. Fresh and dried flowers in olive oil are used to treat painful joints and swellings. A cooled infusion makes a wonderful eye bath for tired and itchy eyes, which can prove invaluable for hayfever sufferers on days when the pollen count is high.

Camomile infusions are often used to bathe wounds and sores, when the anti-inflammatory properties of the plant come into their own. These same properties make it a useful tea in cases of cystitis and kidney inflammation. It promotes the flow of urine and reduces fluid retention.

Rinsing your hair with an infusion of camomile is a cheap and effective way of creating golden locks – this particular method was in practice long before peroxide was used to bleach the hair! Children have a particular affinity with camomile, as it is so gentle and healing. Colic, teething pains and infantile convulsions can all be aided. In a situation where a child is restless and fractious, cooled camomile tea can have a positive soothing effect. It is also one of the most potent of cures for nightmares, in children and adults alike. It is used to dispel tension, fear and emotional distress from the past, aiding emotional stability.

The essential oil of camomile is a useful oil to have around the home. Camomile essential oil is captured by steam distillation of the flower head and has a sweet, strong smell. In this form, it makes an excellent skincare oil and diluted in a carrier oil can be used in cases of acne, allergies, burns, eczema, dermatitis, psoriasis and inflamed skin conditions. If you find yourself flying off the handle before your period, try massaging your abdomen with diluted camomile essential oil to relax and comfort. Camomile flowers can be added to salads and desserts, though the sweet smell masks a rather bitter taste, they make lovely decoration.

Suppliers

Neal's Yard Remedies
Suppliers of essential oils, flower and herbal remedies as well as a range of ingredients and equipment for making your own natural remedies.
www.nealsyardremedies.com
Tel: +44 (0)845 262 3145

Culpeper
Suppliers of natural wellbeing products such as essential oils, carrier oils, natural baby care and natural beauty products.
www.culpeper.co.uk
Tel: +44 (0)1451 822681

Napiers
Complementary health clinics and suppliers natural health care products.
www.napiers.net
Tel: +44 (0) 131 343 3292

Useful Websites

The National Institute of Medical Herbalists
www.nimh.org.uk
Tel: +44 (0) 1392 426022
E-mail: info@nimh.org.uk
Elm House, 54 Mary Arches Street, Exeter, EX4 3BA

Green Events
www.greenevents.co.uk
E-mail: london@greenevents.co.uk
PO Box 104, Lewes, Sussex, BN7 9AX